MW00978109

AN ATHEIST GUIDE TO GOD

SOPHIA O. Y. JONES

An Atheist Guide To God
by Sophia O. Y. Jones

Printed in the United States of America

ISBN 978-1-60647-352-8

www.xulonpress.com

To: Cindy's baby
FAVORITE
Sister

-2009-

Dad, Cinny's
Favorite
sister
Good

DEDICATION

I would like to dedicate this book, to my late great grandma Icilda Duncan and my late grandma Rachael McGhan. They both have sacrificed tremendously for me. It is never too late to say, "Thank you and I love you."

TABLE OF CONTENTS

INTRODUCTION

I was taking a class called, Intro to Evangelism, where I was faced with the task to write my testimony. The guidelines were read and I thought that they were too restrictive. We had to write four paragraphs, and when recited, it should be completed within a minute and a half. It was one of the most difficult and thought provoking task I had to do.

A rough draft was completed and taken to class. Then, I was the first volunteer to stand up and recite my testimony. To my surprise, there were a lot of criticisms.

My instructor told me to take out the negatives and said, "If I was a non-Christian, I would not be able to understand you. Don't get me wrong! I fully understand what you are trying to say, but you have to make it, so that a Christian and a non-Christian can understand what you are trying to say."

Then, one of my classmates blurted out something that I would never forget.

She said, "MAKE IT PLAIN!"

I went home that night feeling puzzled. I thought it was presented in a way, which was easily understood. I sat down to re-write a rough draft, but the three words from my classmate kept repeating itself in my mind.

"MAKE IT PLAIN!"

The following week, I took the rough draft to class but it felt as if, it was incomplete. After class, I took it to the same instructor and then he referred me to the other instructor. She was absent on the day of the first recital. There she was, standing over the desk, so I walked towards her and asked if my testimony was up to standards. She took the papers, placed it on the desk, traced it word for word with her index finger, and read it in a low soft voice.

Suddenly! Her language changed from English to something incomprehensible, yet she continued to trace the words with her finger. Feeling fearful, I wanted to run out of the room, but I stood my ground staring at her in shock. My whole body felt as if it froze temporarily.

I remember thinking to myself, "She must be speaking in Tongues. How can she read, speak in Tongues and understand the text?"

Feeling rejected, I thought it was impossible for her to respond to my question. Yet, she flipped the page, continued to trace the words with her finger, while speaking in a different language to the end.

Finally, she looked up at me. Then she spoke in English with a normal tone, as if nothing strange occurred.

"Honey, I don't see anything wrong with it; you just have to explain yourself. What do you mean by physical?" she asked.

"It means, I can only rely on the things that I can see," I responded.

"Well, write it down, the way you just explained it to me!" she responded.

I think she was referring to the last paragraph I had written stating, "I am no longer a physical being, but a spiritually molded being through Jesus Christ."

I gathered up my things, pretended that I did not witness anything out of the norm and went home. I thought that writing something about my life was going to be an easy task. Little did I know, it was going to be a spiritual process.

I started on another rough draft again but there was a mental block, so I lay down on my bed and closed my eyes.

I ask myself over and over again, "How can I make it plain?"

Out of nowhere, I heard a voice said, "You were an Atheist!"

I was startled, because it was not of my own thought. My eyes opened, glanced around the room, then towards the window, as if I was expecting to find an intruder. There was no one in the room but me. Even if it was of my own thought, it had to be my little secret.

I pondered the thought, "After all, I am now a Christian that was an embarrassing episode in my life. I cannot write down that at one point in my life, I believed that there was no God."

Calling myself or repeating the word "Atheist," caused my body to shriek, as if I had an allergic reaction. The word gave me a scare.

Then, I heard the voice again saying, "You were an Atheist, plain and simple!"

In my mind I was responding, "That is too harsh!"

"When you were in high school, while you were taking biology you didn't think I existed. When you joined the Navy, you wrote no religious preference. Who do you think gave you your great grandma and who do you think got you into that school in the Navy," asked the voice?

"How did you know that?" I wondered.

I was reminded of things that happened in my life that no one knew except for me. Then, I realized where the source came from.

It was as if I saw flashing episodes of my life and I thought, "Oh my God! It is you! You were with me the whole entire time."

I was forced to look back at my life and the fact of the matter was; I was an Atheist. There was no other choice but to be obedient to the voice that challenged me, so I re-wrote the first and last paragraph of my testimony. This is what I wrote in its exact words.

"I was a former atheist set out on a personal conquest to disprove the existence of God. If I could not touch it, hear it, taste it, smell it, or feel it, it did not exist.

I felt the need to become a Christian when one weekend, I visited my mom and she invited me to go to church. I remember her being very prissy and probably wouldn't be caught dead making a public spectacle of herself. The pastor was preaching and asked, "Can I get a witness." My mom jumped up and said, "Yea!" real loud, not once but twice. I was so-oo shocked, that I expressed my surprise to her, so she witness to me. It changed my life and brings me one-step closer to God.

I became a Christian at the age of 14, but backslide due to lack of knowledge. Last year I moved back home and my mom invited me to church, I turned her down until she Announced it was, "dress down month" It appealed to me, so I made up my mind that I was going to attend the whole month. Each week the message became clearer and clearer, then without a shadow of a doubt, I rededicated my life to Jesus Christ once more.

Now Jesus is everything to me. I realize that how could a highly sophisticated specialized being just appear by some biochemical accident? I decided spiritually through Jesus Christ, the unseen, unsung hero who created us by, "letting go and let God, just simply believing, fueled by faith." Now my personal conquest is to challenge any atheist who disproves the theory of God.

After the spring semester, we had the summer off. With nothing to do, I remember my instructor urging us to read our Bibles. Cheating, I flipped to the last chapter, starting with the book of Revelation. It left a bad taste in my mouth. Feeling frustrated, I went to the New Testament.

One day I was meditating and the voice came back to me again saying, "Remember when you said that you wanted to write a book, but you wanted to preserve your integrity."

"Yes!"I answered in the form of a thought.

"Well, why don't you write me a book called, 'An Atheist Guide to God'?"

"An Atheist Guide to God' that is a harsh title! Who will buy such a book? People will avoid such a title!" I protested.

The response was, "Write the title as is, plain and simple."

I did say that I wanted to write a book, but that was a long time ago. I have always wanted to write a book, but I had a mental block. It was easy for me to write about romance, but I stayed clear from that route. I wanted to write a book of substance. I felt the need to be obedient, so I accepted the challenge.

During this time, I came up with a business idea and I told a couple of people. Then one day, I received a phone call with someone selling me the same idea. Even though I was disappointed, I bought the plan anyway. With a new project in my life, it was difficult to focus on one.

Finally, I set aside one weekend to write, when I was interrupted to go shopping. We were driving by the land that our new church was going to be built. As we drove by, the land was bare and inactive, with no equipments indicating a start.

I said in anger. "I thought they said that they were going to start to build the church? There are no equipments, not even a pitch fork and they are collecting our money. This is ridiculous!"

I was in a bad mood, by the time we reached our destination. The rest of my time was spent being overly critical and impatient. As soon as I got home, I went to my room, and made an attempt to write again. Immediately, I felt as if something left my body. It was as if I had an inner core that pried itself away from me. I was startled! The feeling was so abrupt, leaving me to feel empty, lonely and sad. Instantly, I noticed a difference. My behavior pattern changed and my inner peace was gone.

I asked myself, "What is going on? I feel lonely and sad, but I am not lonely and sad."

I tried to ignore my feelings and continued to write. Doing the best that I could, I thought that I had completed a whole chapter. Counting the pages, I realized that I needed more and this was only the handwritten version. There were only four pages, I wanted to quit.

Out of no where, there was a voice in a mocking tone saying, "Ha, ha! You don't even have enough words to write a book. I don't even know why you want to write a book anyway. If I were you I would give up. You don't even have enough words."

Feeling discouraged, I thought about it, "How can I write this book and I don't know enough about God or the Bible? I am not a Bible scholar."

I did not feel like writing any more, but I still felt sad, lonely and miserable. Wanting to escape this feeling, I called up a couple of friends whom I treated like my sisters and offer to take them to the movies. While on our way to the movie theater, the feeling lingers. I told them both that I did not feel right and I did not know what is happening to me. Therefore, I prayed out loud for an edge of protection from all harm and danger. We arrived safely, got our tickets and were seated.

At approximately three quarters into the movie, the same nagging voice came back again saying, "I think your phone is bugged. How did they find out about your business idea, and then sell it back to you? You are not saving any money because you are giving it away to the church."

While being bombarded with negativity, I started to agree with my adversary and felt as if something held my heart and squeezed harder and harder each time the voice scolded me. The pain was so sharp that I was literally gasping for air. Slowly, I slouched downward in the chair from the excruciating pain. Trying to call out for help, I could hardly talk. When I tried to inhale, it literally hurt to breathe.

I looked to the side to try and tell the kids that I could not breathe, but they were so engrossed in the movie. I looked to the other side and everyone was looking at the screen. Besides, it was dark in the theater.

Stricken and paralyzed I could not breathe, talk or move. To make matters worst, I could not communicate to anyone how I was feeling or to have someone call for an ambulance. Feeling desperation; the only thing left was death. I fought back by holding my breath, trying not to inhale or move. If I did, I would have absorbed a massive blow to my heart. All I could do was to sit still and call out for Jesus.

Then I heard another voice said, "My sheep will know my voice. My sheep will know my voice and the voice of a stranger it will not follow."

I knew what that meant, so I immediately placed my hand on my chest and said, "I rebuke you satan in the name of Jesus. You have no power or authority over me. This is private property; take your hands off my heart."

The pain went away and I was able to breathe again. I could not believe it. No one saw me struggling.

I looked over at the kids and said, "Didn't you guys see me gasping for air, I almost died?"

They gave me this puzzled look and said, "No! Are you alright?"

I responded, "I have to get out of here! Something strange is happening to me. Meet me outside."

My heart still felt heavy, so I went into the car and prayed the pain away. Usually, I am a positive person with inner strength and mental stability. I try my best, not to let anyone or anything get to me. First, I opened the door by displaying negative attitudes. Second, I was attacked mentally, making me doubt myself and others. Third, I was physically attacked.

From that time onward, I realized that there was a calling on my life, to open the eyes of those who are blinded from the truth. It was not child's play anymore. I had to take my spiritual blinders off. What happened to me inside the movie theater was not an accident. It only made me stronger, with a special need to complete my assigned task.

> "For though we walk in the flesh, we do not war after the flesh: (For our weapons of warfare are not carnal, but mighty through God to the pulling down of strong holds;) Casting down imagination, and every high thing that exalteth itself against the knowledge of God, and bringing into captivity every thought to the obedience of Christ; (2 Corinthians 10:3-5) KJV

My brothers and sisters, it is time for us to unveil the curtains of ignorance and acknowledge the unseen forces that resides with us, in us and around us. It amuses me to see people looking and searching in outer space, asking if we are alone. Absolutely not! The fact of the matter is; it is not visible to the naked eyes.

What if I was to tell you, that each individual is under surveillance 24 hours a day, 7 days a week, and 365 days throughout the year, by these same unseen forces? They can see us but we cannot see them, with the capability of entering our thoughts, imaginations and dreams. Please join me on this journey, in our quest to find God.

CHAPTER ONE

YOU MIGHT BE AN ATHEIST

An Atheist is an Atheist not of choice but is a victim of circumstance, which one can equate for having book sense and lacking commonsense. Book sense is processing information gained from others with or without merit using memorization, therefore limiting our ability to separate facts from fiction. Common sense is processing information in the form of waste management, using our intellect therefore eliminating facts from fiction. Book sense minus commonsense is equal to nonsense. Book sense plus commonsense is equal to a sixth sense. This is a vital asset an Atheist lacks to process information sensibly.

In my twenties, I had strong views and was very opinionated. One day while working together with my mother, we got into a heated discussion. Being young and brass, I thought I was knowledgeable and versatile because I was well read. I cherished the rights to freedom of speech and often tortured my mom with outrageous statements. Therefore, I said something to provoke her.

My mom sat back, continued doing what she was doing and said in a quiet precise tone, "He who knows not, and knows not that he knows not, is a fool. Shun him."

My first thought was, "Did Mother just called me a fool?"

The second thought, "I should be insulted."

The third thought, "You need a quick response."

The Fourth thought, "What was that statement?"

Then the fifth thought, "What a powerful quote!"

Usually, I have a quick response, but I became entangled in my thoughts. I was so-OO impressed that I asked her to repeat it once again. She repeated the quote, and this time she added the rest.

"He who knows not, and knows not that he knows not is a fool. Shun him. He who knows not, and knows that he knows not, is a child. Teach him. He who knows, and knows not that he knows, is asleep. Wake him. He who knows, and knows that he knows is a leader. Follow him."

Omar Khayam, 13th century philosopher

Mother lashed me verbally and it was the best insult I've ever had. Back then I had the wrong ideas and concepts. I never thought about, how the consequence of my own personal thoughts and opinions, could have an impact on me, others and the environment.

Then an instructor told me not to challenge what I was taught. He alluded to the fact that my grades would excel, on the basis of my exact replica of the text. Another instructor told me the story of his college experience. He told me that his roommate was highly intelligent, who refused to duplicate the author's views. His instructors failed him. Therefore, he had to repeat a couple of classes or else he could not graduate from college.

We are taught to duplicate man-made theories as facts, while there is a bias against the teachings of the Bible. Is it the Bible and its messages or the individuals who use it to prey on those who are ignorant of its messages?

A psychotic picks apart its verses to rectify their cause. The con artist distorts its verses in hopes to gain. Certain regimes ban its contents, so the people serve them instead of God. An intellectual reads its contents yet they do not understand. Most people don't read it, so you can use its words to manipulate them. Then the Atheist uses it to blame God.

"What a powerful Book!" Aren't you curious as to why an Atheist wants to take its Words out of circulation? You can separate church from state, but you cannot separate God from state. Church is church and God is, period.

Those who fail to recognize the fact that there is a God, usually have an intense feeling of neglect from the Creator, due to lack of knowledge. I cannot stress enough that misguidance and ignorance will cripple your mind, leaving you defenseless. The belief in God is diminishing at an alarming rate. Now that I know that there is a God. I am humbled by the experience.

The thing I fear the most about writing this book, is plagiarism. I am trying my very best to acknowledge and give credit to quotes and phrases, which are not of my own. It bothers me a great deal. Yet, we are born into this world with all its originality and benefits. Then, we fail to acknowledge and give credit to its original Creator, who is the rightful owner.

Do you ever wonder, why God had the audacity to request one tenth from us? It is because; He created everything in the Earth, on the Earth and around the Earth. My house, its contents, the car that I drive, the place that I work, the food that I eat, the water that I drink, the clothes that I wear, the shoes on my feet, the jewelry and the very air I breathe is made from God's creation.

What is ironic is the fact that we take from the stuff, in, on and around the Earth, erect a building, calls it a courthouse and acknowledges the Commandments of God. Then a group of individuals thinks that this public building belongs to them, therefore, we ought to remove the Words of God.

God owns one tenth of all buildings erected on this Earth. We as a majority should say, "NO." We should not allow them to take away our blessings and our edge of protection. Lawyers and Supreme Court take note.

I work in a hospital and at times I would see plaques or an entire wing, dedicated to its donors. Yet we take from the Earth and refuse to acknowledge, it's Donor. For every ailment there is an antidote. When we are sick we take medications in all forms, made from the stuff, in, on and around the Earth. Every man-made product should have an insignia stating the fact that it was made from God's creation along with the designer's logo and company name.

"The earth is the Lord's and the fullness thereof; the world and they that dwell therein. For he hath founded it upon the seas, and established it upon the floods." (Psalm 24: 1-2) KJV

I had a strong Christian background, but because of my keen observation through life I became distorted. The thought of uttering and labeling myself as a former Atheist, is still very uncomfortable to me. When I was given the title of this book, I was appalled thinking that no one would pick up a book that refers to them, as being an Atheist. Then it was revealed to me that the majority of us are, and we do not realize it.

Most of us claim to believe in God, yet we do not follow the rules and discipline required for a sacred life. Most of us who attend church on a regular basis do not read our Bibles. The only means of spiritual growth is what we hear from the pulpit.

If you do not read your Bible, how can you be fed a proper nutritional diet to maintain spiritual growth? We are both physical and spiritual beings.

If you do not understand, you cannot begin to grasp the basic concept of, "Who you are?"

When I refer to us as physical beings, it means that we can use our five senses to define our existence. When I refer to us as spiritual beings, it means that we are connected to an unseen source that is a direct tie to our existence. This completes the whole.

The Bible said, "Man shall not live by bread alone, but by every word that proceedeth out of the mouth of God." (Matthew 4:4) KJV

This means that in order for us to have a balance diet, we need both physical and spiritual food. Physically, our bodies need food in the form of nutrients, where it is chewed, swallowed, processed, absorbed, transported, stored and excreted. Did you notice, when we are infants, nutrition is an important factor? We could not eat just any type of food. If we lack a specific nutrient, more than likely it could lead to blindness and other forms of abnormalities.

Spiritually, our body needs food to feed the soul. The Bible provides us with a vast menu of spiritual food. Literally speaking, the Words of the Bible are food. When you partake of this essential nutrient, our bodies act like a satellite dish, which connects us to the unseen Source that is responsible for us being here. That source is God, who created our very being.

"Now we have received, not the spirit of the world, but the spirit which is of God, that we might know the things that are freely given to us of God. Which things also we speak, not in the words which man's

wisdom teacheth, but which the Holy Ghost teacheth; comparing spiritual things with spiritual. But the natural man receiveth not the things of the Spirit of God: for they are foolishness unto him: neither can he know them, because they are spiritually discerned.
I Corinthians (2:12-14) KJV

If you starve yourself, physically the body slowly deteriorates then you die. Can you imagine what type of damage is done, when one lacks spiritual food? We become basically blind with lots of abnormalities in our behavior patterns. Therefore, we cannot fully utilize the Source, thinking that it is non-existent, because we cut off its supply. Most of us are running around blind, thinking there is no God. You are right; there is no God, because you are spiritually dead.

If your body is deteriorating, somewhere out there, a prey is waiting. At the first sign of weakness, they want to devour your flesh and pick your bones clean. Can you imagine what happens to you spiritually? As there are physical preys, so are there spiritual preys in the form of demonic forces. When we cut off the source of God, we fall prey to evil sources. This is very evident in our society.

We spend billions of dollars on defense, not to mention outer space, where there is surveillance. We all want to know if we are the only civilization that exists. Some of us are worried about an alien invasion. I hate to be the bearer of bad news, but in case you did not notice, we have already been invaded by unseen sources. Judging by the evidence, it has demonic connotations written all over it.

How do you think these sources breech the security of our highly sophisticated equipments? It is time for us to change the way we think and act, so that we can connect ourselves back to the source of God. The Words that proceeded out of the mouth of God are captured and stored in the Bible. It is essential as the air we breathe to sustain life. With the

Words of God you have power, authority and victory over these seen and unseen demonic spirits.

I cannot believe how blind I was; to me God did not exist. I searched all over not realizing that I had an improper diet and shut God off. Being ignorant is not an excuse any more. Then, we wonder why the moral fiber of this entire earth is deteriorating. I love people with all my heart that is why I took the time out to write this book, because I did not have to. Well, in a sense I have to.

My job is not to judge you, but to tell you the truth. I am a mere messenger filled with imperfections. Please do not be offended. You might be saying, "We are only human, and we make mistakes."

This is the biggest illusion orchestrated by mankind, for lack of courtesy, love, respect, empathy, kindness, loyalty, morals, courage, knowledge, wisdom, understanding, strength, justice, peace, patience, honesty, unity, friendship, compassion, etc. Instead of changing for the good, we are becoming accustomed to accepting a lawless way of life. Making excuses for the way we use and abuse each other.

I found myself falling into the same way of thinking and accepting. We use to be polite to each other. Now, we practically run each other over without apologizing. What is going on? As we loose our conscience, we loose our respect for life.

> Jesus said, "Not everyone that saith unto me, Lord, Lord shall enter into the kingdom of heaven; but he that doeth the will of my father which is in heaven. Many will say to me in that day, Lord, Lord, have we not prophesied in thy name? and in thy name have cast out devils? and in thy name done many wonderful works? And then will I profess unto them, I never knew you: depart from me, ye that work iniquity. Matthew (7:21-23)

Most of us go to church practically every Saturday or Sunday and sometimes during the week, yet we are not connected to the source of God. In other words we are connected to another source.

Some of us lead dual lives, one for society and one for the church environment. Instead of forgiving and forgetting, we become entrapped in bitterness and hate. If you cannot forgive or show mercy to your fellowmen, why should God extend that open invitation to you?

You could read your Bible everyday, feed the hungry, and help the misfortunate. Remember no one is perfect, and I know without a doubt that you have done things in your life that you are not proud of. If you hold a grudge against your brothers and sisters, so will the Lord.

You can start now by asking the Lord to forgive you and forgive others that mistreated you. Respond with empathy, no one can tell me that they have never talked about or mistreated anyone. I remember being very upset, angry and hurt when I was talked about; when in actuality I did the same thing to others. Yet, we continue to do the same things.

The self professed Atheist is not the one, I am most concerned about. It is the religious Atheist that is of most concern. The ones who claim to believe in God and privately they lack the knowledge, wisdom and understanding of the true God. Therefore, we create a system where the blind is leading the blind.

Why was the Atheist able to get the law in their favor to remove God's Ten Commandments from a court house? Most of the laws were adopted from the Bible to begin with; therefore it is very appropriate to have the ultimate law displayed. While our representatives of God lie dormant with the inability to stop the attacks and demise of the Principles of God. Why is that? Then, the church with its entire member did not take a stand, marched or protested.

Why should they denounce the Atheist when they themselves do not have the Ten Commandments posted in their
place of worship? If you take a survey of the self professed
people of God, you will be surprised to know the majority
do not know the Ten Commandments. Then, there are some
of us who thinks the laws should be changed to adapt to our
lifestyle. Shouldn't it be the other way around? We are the
ones who should be changing our lifestyle to adapt to the
law.

If you don't post them, how will people know them? I
wonder why we all lack morals. Some will argue the fact that
Jesus died for all of our sins and it is a sealed deal, therefore
the Ten Commandments are no longer applicable. Instead,
they search for loop holes in the Bible to justify their malad-
justed behavior patterns. The fact is what did the Word of
God stated and not what man thinks it should state?

Isn't this ironic, some say that the Bible was written by
man, but when you think about it. Man would have never
written anything that would make themselves accountable
for their behavior.

"For the prophesy came not in old time by the will of
man: but holy men of God spake as they were moved
by the Holy Ghost. (2 Peter 1:21) KJV

Be very careful that you do not exalt or worship the
creation over the Creator. They are God's representatives,
not his replacement or substitution. Therefore, when you get
mislead, abused or taken advantage of, don't blame God.
You should not put your trust in man. The more naïve you
are about God and his principles the more prone you are of
being taken advantage of.

That is why the Ten Commandments are very important. I do not know if you notice, that each time we break

a commandment, we cause a major catastrophe. It not only affects us, it affects others.

For example, you are married with children and you have an affair. You might or might not have told the person you had the affair with that you were married. Even if the person did not tell you that they were married. The fact of the matter is the Bible warns us of the dangers of fornication. Therefore, you had an affair that could destroy the lives of many.

The person's spouse could be told or they would find out for themselves about the affair. They end up fighting over the whole ordeal; the kids are affected because they have to live in a negative environment. Their parents end up getting a divorce. Then, there is a fight to see who gets them.

Now, they are without guidance, due to the fact that they end up with only one parent. Then, the single parent has to work double time to provide for their children financially. If the parents are not around to teach them right from wrong, the relationship will be emotionally and physically unstable. This is the perfect example of the anatomy and physiology of the demoralization of the human species.

The spouse that had the affair, would probably enter into another relationship, and cannot give of themselves, due to financial obligation to the previous family. Some will not obligate that financial responsibility, then the child or children suffers because a Commandment was broken and the other partner could not forgive. The end result is a continuous cycle of moral deterioration, which leads to destruction. Therefore, we do not live in peace.

The most startling fact is that we blame things on God, and He did not have anything to do with it. My brothers and sisters we are the problem. Take an honest look at ourselves. Do you think God wants a roommate of our caliber to enter into His Kingdom of Heaven? Why do you think God is adamant about righteousness? Do you think it's because He wants to make life difficult for us and ruin our fun?

Heaven is God's domain, not only was it created for Him; it was created for His people. Most of us complain about the unstable ways of life. Sometimes life can stick it to you and make you wish you were never born. Be honest, aren't we the ones who are creating hell on Earth, by our mere disobedience? Then, we have the nerve to complain. This is why God created Heaven, so that we can live in peace.

God is adamant about righteousness, because He will go through any length to protect His sheep. He will sift and sort, conquer and divide, test and try, to make sure that we have peace and joy with eternal life. What is the purpose of having eternal life, if you cannot live it in peace?

Some people have the ideal vision of a perfect world; thinking that we should get rid of other's who do not fall into the mold. If they do not look like us, talk like us, act like us, or beg to differ. They are placed under great scrutiny which resulted in slavery, the holocaust, genocide, ethnic cleansing and war.

There are always some sick, mere mortal men, who think that God gave them the authority to make that judgment. When you take a look at their life, they are far from being perfect. Wait until they find out that they are excluded from the perfect world. If you are a victim or a prey, revenge and judgment belongs to God.

God's adversary was kicked out of Heaven, because he could not follow rules and regulations. His ideals were like a disease spreading and contaminating the Kingdom of Heaven. Now, we are contaminated through Adam and Eve via sin. Sometimes, we can't help the way we act and say the things we say, because we are contaminated. This is how the adversary gets back at God. Rules and regulation is not a part of his nature; his job is to plant a seed of destruction. He knows that God frowns upon sin.

If you have a disease in your body, you have to contain, confine and destroy it before it spread and contaminate everything. If you let it spread, it contaminates everything, which leads to death. For example the Bible tells the story of Noah's Ark. God attempted to contain, confine and destroy the disease of sin. He isolated Noah and his family with a pair of each animal in the Ark. The rest of the Earth was destroyed by water. It was a new beginning for mankind, but man did not change from their wicked ways. The disease survived. So what greater love is it, that as a last resort, God gave us an alternative route?

"For God so love the world, that he gave his only begotten Son, that whosoever believeth in him should not perish, but have everlasting life." (John 3:16) KJV

My brothers and sisters, I am going to take you on a journey in a quest to find God and save our souls. Therefore, we can have eternal life and be roommates in the Kingdom of Heaven.

CHAPTER TWO

ASSIGNING THE BLAME

When I first came to the realization of who I was, I was living in a one room wooden house. It was so small that the length and width of the bed was almost the size of the entire house. The roof was made with several thin sheets of aluminum, to cover its wooden frame.

When you exit through the door, to the right was a built on kitchen. It was encircled with a patchwork of aluminum sheets, stained with rust. Outside of the kitchen, was one water tap used to catch water in containers for kitchen and household needs.

To the left of the house was a built on shower stall, with no roof. The door was tattered from the excessive moisture that eats away at its wooden fiber. Next to the shower stall, was an outdoor toilet with no plumbing? Behind the house was a huge plum tree that hovered over the house, which was a favorite spot for croaking lizards.

During the day, the small lizards were visible so you know how to avoid them. At nights, you could hear them descending upon the roof. As they jumped off the plum tree, their feet made an impact on the roof. With the hollow wooden house and tin roof, the least of all sounds amplified.

It was so-OO clear; you could hear their little feet walking around as they croaked in a menacing tone.

One night, I remember waking up screaming and wriggling, motioning in deep distress, brushing my body off with my hands. It felt as if, they were literally in the room and was crawling all over my body. My great grandma lifted me up, wrapped me in a bundle, grabbed her little bench and hurried outside into the darkness of the night.

We sat in the middle of the yard while she rocked me and repeated the entire 27th Psalms.

> "The Lord is my light and my salvation, whom shall I fear. The Lord is the strength of my life of whom shall I be afraid. When the wicked even mine enemies and my foes, came upon me to eat up my flesh. They stumbled and fell. Thou an host should encamp against me my heart shall not fear. Thou war should rise up against me, in this will I be confident..."

She recited it with such power and authority that I too became empowered. I listened keenly as the crickets played me a lullaby and I drifted off to sleep. After that I could sleep peacefully at nights.

To make matters worst, mosquitoes used me as their pincushion. The more they bit me, the more I scratched and the more I scratched my entire legs were covered with sores. In the mornings I would literally have to peel myself from off the sheets, because my sores adhere themselves to it. Most of my early years were plagued with all kinds of childhood ailments. My great grandma prayed and nursed me back to health.

There was this young lady who would visit on occasion and she was always nicely dressed. I came to know her as my real mother. Being very young, my great grandma was the first person I came to realization with. Therefore, I called her, "Mama." I could tell that my mother wanted more control of me, but she seems to be intimidated by my great grandma. If she had to do anything to me or with me, she would have to first ask for permission.

My mother bought me a chamber pot to make sure I was potty trained and everything modern and up to date. She also wanted to pierce my ears, but she had to go through her grandmother with a lot of convincing to do. Being very old fashioned, Grandma wasn't too keen on the idea. My mom was not about to give in and eventually pierced my ears. She chased after the ice truck, numbed my ears with the ice and pierced it with a needle and thread. At that point I was the only one protesting. My aunt had to help hold me down.

Soon the rest of my family members came to live with us and it was getting crowded. Eventually, we moved back to the house where we were living in originally, with everything indoors including plumbing. It wasn't long before I found out why we moved from there in the first place.

The thing I remembered most as a child, was my love for peace. I could sit in a corner all by myself and play all day. The peace that I had was calm, soothing and secure. It was like having the sensation of weightlessness and if you surrender in its arms, you could grow wings and fly. As I grew older and older the more I tried to hold on to that peace, the more it grew lesser and lesser. If I was in my own little world and someone disrupts it without due cause, I became angry.

I was christened as a Protestant and attended a prep school affiliated with the church. Even though I was raised in a religious environment, no one forced religion on me. In other words, I was raised as an independent thinker. My great grandma did not force me at nights to pray, she prayed out loud enough so that everyone in the household could hear her.

Saying I love you, hugs and kisses were never a part of her raising us, neither were we concerned. She didn't have to tell us anything; we automatically knew and felt the love. She led by example.

Most of my free time was spent at political rallies, going to funerals, attending meetings or special visits to friends and families. I have made my way through crowds and met former and present Prime Ministers at that time by age 13, with a simple handshake. Everywhere my great grandma went she took me with her.

I developed a love for politics, and wanted to change the world I live in. One day, I heard the newspaper man riding through the neighborhood and because of my interest in the world around me; I asked if I could have a newspaper. Before I knew it, my great grandma ran to get her purse as the paper man rode by our house on his bicycle. She zipped pass me and took off running down the street after him. It took him awhile to hear the neighbors trying to stop him.

I felt bad as I watched her ran down the street after him because of her age. To make matters worse the neighbors saw her handing me the newspaper when she returned. They thought I was spoiled rotten. The next time he slowed down and stopped at our gate.

As I became aware of my surrounding, I would also listen to the news. Death, war and violence seem to be the main topic on a global scale.

I thought to myself, "How stupid, why would anyone want to fight and kill each other, is there anything wrong with wanting peace?"

One Sunday, I went to church and heard a sermon on faith.

The pastor said, "Faith in God can move a mighty mountain."

I went home and pondered the thought, "You mean if I pray and ask God for anything and have faith it will be done, great!"

I decided to test my faith. World peace was on the agenda, but I wanted some form of physical evidence. I thought about the mountain in the distant background where I lived.

It was time to go to bed, so I knelt down, clasp my hands and prayed, "Lord please let there be world peace. I am going to go to bed and when I wake up in the morning and listen to the news, I don't want to hear that anyone died from violence. Also, I want the mountain in the background to move."

I went to bed, thinking and believing in peace and that the mountain would move. The next day I awoke and gingerly crawled out of bed to see what the results were. I turned on the radio and the war continued in certain foreign countries and we had some deaths locally. I felt disappointed, and then I remembered the mountain and hurried to see the result. The mountain did not move. That was the first time I prayed and asked for something specific. There were no results.

I said to myself, "Why should I pray to a God, who cannot answer my prayers."

I felt betrayed, the Pastor said, "Faith in God can move a mighty mountain and if I have faith and wanted anything, pray, and it will be done.

Most of the Bible was written in parables. It means that a simple story is introduced, with the same meaning, so that the listener or reader can understand. So when the term, "Faith in God can move a mighty mountain," was introduced to me. I took it literally for its text or what was said. The term actually means that, if there is an obstacle in your way, it could be a person, place or thing. If you have faith and ask the Lord to deliver you, He will provide a way out.

My request to move the mountain was ignorant. Can you imagine if it was moved? Where would it go? Thousands of people would have died, not to mention the plants, animals and properties that would be destroyed. Suppose the mountain was preventing the sea from entering the island, and it was moved. It would have been a major catastrophe.

We need to analyze the situation, before we make any request, which could cause our own disposition. From that day on, I prayed only when I thought it was necessary to pray. This is the perfect example of lack of knowledge. I blamed it on God. I would cry endlessly, when I saw starving children, homelessness and innocent lives taken. It didn't make any sense to me.

You might be saying, "Why does God allow this to happen?"

"For we war not against flesh and blood, but against principalities, against powers, against the rulers of darkness of this world, against spiritual wickedness in high places." (Ephesians 6:12) KJV

The adversary and one third of the angels fell from glory. They are the spiritual vultures I was writing about. Their job is to conceal the truth and lead us all astray. These spiritual vultures know that God loves us and they use us as shields. For God to destroy them, He would have to destroy us to get to them. Therefore, God have to save us on an individual basis, through Jesus.

My brothers and sisters, we are the ones who gave them the power and authority to rule the earth, through spiritual deficiency. Instead of being connected to the source of God, some are connected to spiritual preys.

This is why an Atheist is so easy to be manipulated. Whenever they see or hear the word God or Jesus they cringe as if they had an allergic reaction. They want to take the name out of circulation.

"Why do we have to have the Ten Commandments displayed, God on our money, my kid reciting it at school, take it off our public buildings, etc. etc.?"

Stop impeding on others life! If you want God out of your life, I respect your choice. If you know that you are ignorant of facts, do not make a decision for the whole. Think before you act!

Do you think that if you take God out of everything, the world will be a better place and we will live in peace forever? Think again genius, unless it is your objective and will to work for the enemy. Congratulations on your task of going to court and winning your rights to freedom of ignorance!

I remember the first fight I got into, it was a lesson I will never forget. A bunch of us kids were playing, and I got into a verbal confrontation with an individual.

The others noticed and said, "Are you going to let her talk to you like that?"

I looked at my friends and they stared at me. The issue turned into a matter of pride as I responded with an insult. They loved my response, as they gathered around us and attracted others. The next thing I know was my opponent and I were facing each other with both of our chest rising and falling at a rapid pace. We were staring each other down, while the crowd encouraged us to fight. Neither of us wanted to fight, but we were surrounded by a thirsty audience that gathered to see a fight.

One of my friends went and picked up a mango seed and a piece of charcoal and came in between the both of us. She drew a line in between us and positioned her body so that the only thing between us was her hand. She placed the mango seed on the palm of her outstretched hand and shook it up, down and all around.

"Hot patty, hot patty the baddest one knocks the mango seed out of my hand, cross the line, and touch a button."

I knew what that meant, so I looked around and saw several members of her family in the crowd. I told them that I was not going to fight her because they were there. They just assured me that they would not allow it to happen. There I was, entrapped and assured with no place to escape. I thought that I could defeat her, so I knock the mango seed out of the hand, cross the line and slightly touched my opponent.

With all the commotion and excitement generated by the crowd, I lost my concentration. My opponent pounced on me like a cat and I fell to the ground, as she continued to scratch my face and rip my clothes to shreds. I was so shocked that I could not defend myself. It happened so fast.

Finally, someone pulled her off of me. When I looked down I noticed that my dress was ripped. Feeling humiliated I quickly gathered the torn fabric, which was still attached to cover myself. I got up, went into my house and started to cry.

My great grandma saw me and asked, "What happened? Look at your face and clothes!"

Expecting sympathy I responded pitifully, "Barbara, beat me up and ripped my clothes.".

"What! Wait until I see her mother, I am going to...," as she grabbed my hands and headed towards the gate.

I tried to keep her inside, "Wait! Hold on a minute! I'm all right. Please don't go out there and say anything!"

"What! After she beat you up like that. Come on, let's go!" She pulled me towards her house.

My hands tried to grasp at anything that could prevent me from going back outside, but I was separated from them all including the gate. Most of the crowd was still there, arguing over the fact. Apparently, there were some adults; trying to find out how did such a thing took place? I tried to free my arms, all I wanted to do was to run back into the house and hide my face, but I had a dead grip around my wrist. My great grandma parted the crowd and we saw Barbara's older sister responding to the accusations.

"Look what your little sister did to my grand-daughter! You guys are going to have to pay for this," my granny interrupted, as she pointed to my dress, while my head hung low.

"Sophia started it!" said one of her family members.

"That's a lie!" blurted one out of the crowd.

Half the people said I did it and half said she did it. Barbara did the smart thing, she was no where to be found. She was then called by her older sister to join us outside. She came outside and gave her version, that I started it.

"That's a lie!" I protested.

"If you think that I am lying ask Kizzy," said Barbara.

Kizzy was the one who drew the line and had the mango seed in her hand, she was also missing. The crowd went to get her and brought her to us. She had a reputable image, so they asked her who started it. I was sure that she was going to say Barbara, because she was there when it all started. I do not remember quite what happened, but Barbara swore at me and they ask me if I going to let her get away with what she said. I guess she forgot, after all I am the one who knocked the mango seed out of her hand.

"Sophia did," she responded without hesitation.

I could not believe it; my great grandma pulled me away from the crowd. No one admitted that they encouraged us to fight. When I got home I tried to explain how the fight began.

My great grandma said, "You can stay there letting people take you for an idiot or a puppet show, it doesn't matter! You touched her first."

Weeks after the fight, Barbara would still try to intimidate me and I tried all means to avoid her. On another day, Kizzy and I were playing and Barbara showed up trying to impose her will on me. This time I refused. She walked right in my path and was an inch away staring me down with threats. I pushed her away and then she charged back.

She came at me with such force that I fell backwards with her about to land on top of me. This caused me to think real quickly by using my legs to push upward flipping her body in mid air. She had such a harsh landing that it surprised the both of us. By the time I got on my feet, she looked at me petrified and ran away.

After that incident occurred my attitude changed. I was determined not to let any one intimidate me. I made a personal rule. If I did not bother anyone and someone bothered me; I would give them three chances. It didn't have to be anything big, my blood would boil and all hell broke loose. I would literally loose my temper and God bless the individual. I thought that I had all rights and justification to take matters into my own hand.

I use to say that if I was in a court of law and anyone would sit up on the witnesses stand and lied on me, even if I was in shackles. I would break free and knock some truth into them."

I just hated the fact that someone would lie, bother or say negative things about me, especially if I did not do them anything. That was the most low down, dirty thing anyone could do to a person.

One day I was asked to do something by an adult in my household. I didn't like the way I was asked, so I said I was not going to do it unless I was asked properly. It turned into an argument, as I tried to let that adult know that common courtesy should be used. The more I defended myself, the more that adult sent out a range of verbal assaults that was totally unnecessary. This adult thought it was beneath her to say, please to a nine year old.

"You shouldn't say those things, she is just a child. Further more she is right, you should say please," interrupted my grandma.

"I am not going to, who the hell she think she is," as she responded with more insults.

My blood began to boil, and everyone know by now that all hell was about to break loose. Everyone was at guard. They know that something was about to happen, but what, they did not know.

My great grandma stood before that adult and me. She knows that I usually kick, throw or break something when deeply agitated. Soon, I lost my temper, as the last words pierced me. I was aware of the fact that I couldn't and wouldn't hit an adult, so I looked around because I had to release this built up rage. I was so angry that if there was a tree, I would have uprooted it.

The only thing in my path was my cousin who was one year younger than I was. I chased towards her, and everyone ran after me. They held me around my waist to try and pull me back as I wrapped my hands around her neck. Soon, they let me go, and attempted to pry my hands from around her neck.

I continued until I heard a voice said, "That's enough Sophia, stop!"

I quickly released my hands, and a feeling of deep regret came over me, because she was totally innocent. My great grandma sat with me as I settled down, then others attended to my cousin. I sat on the bench with my head hung low.

My grandma spoke to me with a soft voice and said, "You know, you could have killed your cousin."

The thought of it send shock waves in my mind, which was not my intention.

"Do you want to go to jail, and never see your family again?"

"No!" I answered with fear.

"Well, don't you ever let anyone, cause you to lose your cool like that again, that you harm anyone. They will always win and you will always lose. Every time you lose your temper, you destroy things. You will end up with nothing if you continue like that. Think before you act, use your intelligence, no one is worth it."

Most often we let people get the best of us, not realizing that they win and we lose in the long run. It is our fault when we allow anyone to cause us to lose our cool. It doesn't matter who started the assaults.

The question is, "Can you maintain the peace or rather do you know how to maintain the peace?"

We blame God saying, "Why does He allow bad things to happen?"

How could I request world peace, when I myself did not know how to maintain the peace? Peace would have lasted less than a day, because no one is willing to sacrifice, we let pride get in the way. One of our greatest faults is that we judge too much, we are always looking at others instead of looking into ourselves. It is easy to find fault in others because we can see them, but we cannot see ourselves.

We do things behind closed doors, thinking no one can see us. Our thoughts alone are a cesspool of waste that could pollute an entire hemisphere. Some of us judge people so much that we become psychotic, intruding on other people's rights and end up sinning ourselves.

One of my favorite stories in the Bible was the woman who was caught in the act of adultery and she was taken to Jesus by her accusers. They told Him about her sin, and then they ask Him what they should do. Jesus ignored them, and acted as if he did not hear. They ask repeatedly.

Jesus responded, "He that is without sin among you, let him first cast a stone at her." (John 8:7) KJV

The people thought about what Jesus said, and no one could say that they were without sin, so they walked away.

One of the most hilarious things is our ignorance. We put everything in categories, that we think we can categorize sin. Do we think that God is going to put us in categories and sentence us to hell for a brief moment, by calling our sin a minor misdemeanor, while people who commit a major sin is sentenced to life in hell. A sin is a sin, no matter what it may be. There is no difference between killing someone and coveting your neighbor's assets.

Most of us probable sin several times a day, and do not know how or why we sin. We are so busy judging others that we think we are sinless. That is why it is so important to forgive others and ask for forgiveness also. I myself is not immune everyday is a constant battle, I have to monitor my thoughts, what I say, my actions and most of all, others.

When I was in high school I wrote this, "Don't get mad or even, preserve your integrity. To fight back is weak; it only means, you are not in control of yourself."

As I journey through life I changed my status, I thought it was a dumb thing to say. I re-discovered it while going through some old writings, now I re-apply it to my own life. We are not in control of ourselves, if we let others get us upset, or drive us into rage.

The sad thing is there are adults who behave like a brat, whose main objective is to get under your skin. Respond with an act of diplomacy; let the individual know that you have better things to do with your life, than to waste precious time arguing over anything meaningless.

Let's face the facts, "What does God have to do with our current situation?"

CHAPTER THREE

FOOLISH PRIDE

It was near dusk and what was left was a peep of light, from the sunset. I was approximately ten years old, playing in the front yard. A shriek of laughter and echoes of jeers stopped us dead in our tracks and pulled our attention to an event that was going on outside the street. My cousins and I ran to the gate, grabbed a designated spot and was looking for some form of entertainment.

There seemed to be a stranger in our neighborhood. He walked and staggered with arms swinging, as if he was swatting flies. The boys in the neighborhood were poking him with sticks. It seemed funny at the time, until I realize that they were trying to get into his pockets. He seemed to be lost for words; all we could hear were solitary moans. My smile turned into a frown. I wanted to tell the boys to stop, but I was too afraid to talk. Finally, I felt the hand of my great grandma on my shoulder, as she leaned forward.

"What are you boys doing? Leave the man alone!" shouted my great grandma.

The boys stopped immediately, while the man staggered towards the voice that rescued him.

I thought to myself, "Why does my great grandma always get us involved?"

I wanted them to stop bothering the man, but I wanted someone else to stop it. Soon the kids in the neighborhood followed him.

I sighed to myself, "Oh no! Now, they are all at our gate."

The speechless stranger managed to utter the words, "Mother, can you please spare me some food?"

My grandma turned to look towards me. As if I knew what she was going to say, I held my head down and said to myself, "Oh, no!"

"Sophia, could you go into the house and get him some food!"

I walked towards the house unwillingly, upset that she got me involved, with the neighborhood kids watching me. When I got into the house, I shared out some food for him, while I looked at them through the window. Judging by his appearance I did not want him to use the same items we ate with, so I found a chipped plate and a fork that was bent.

We had a short wall and a short gate, so he hopped up and sat on the wall with his back turned towards the house. My great grandma also had her back towards the house comforting him.

I picked up the plate on either sides with my thumbs and index finger. As I pushed the door open, I made up my face and hung my pinkie fingers off to the sides. When the kids saw it, they laughed. I guess I was not quick enough, my great grandma's eyes and mine met simultaneously, which made me straightened up my face and put my pinkies down immediately.

As I walked towards them both, her expression changed when she saw the chipped plate and the bent fork. This caused a furious backhand that sent the plate with food crashing to the ground. Standing in place stiffened, I braced myself for what was to come.

"How dare you come out here with your face made up, and your little fingers sprawled out to the sides, thinking you are better than anybody? Look at the chipped up plate and bent up fork. Who do you think you are? Respect is due, even to the common dog!"

The words showered me, as if we had a temporary weather change and the forecast was thunder and lightening with heavy rain. I could still feel her breath on my face. Everyone stood there with a shocked look on their faces, while I hung my face in disgrace, trying not to look at anyone directly.

"Now go inside the house and get a decent plate and fork and fix another plate and when you get back, clean this mess up!"

I turned and hurried into the house. As I looked out the window I saw my cousin attempting to pick up the mess, when she was interrupted.

"Is your name, Sophia?"

"No!" said my petrified cousin.

"Then let her pick it up," answered my upset grandma.

It took me a while to gather enough pride to walk back outside. I was filled with shame and embarrassment. I gave the man the plate of food and quickly ran inside, when I heard her say.

"Where is she? Get out here right now and clean up this mess!"

I went outside slowly, got down on my hands and knees and began to clean up the mess, as the crowd watched on and the man ate as if he was starving. He finished his food and before I had the chance to finish cleaning up, my grandma handed me the empty plate.

I gave her the, "Don't you see I am cleaning up look," but it did not matter.

I took the plate and placed it in the sink and went back outside. One of my friends, covered her mouth, pointed at me and chuckled.

I was totally humiliated. Soon, all interest turned to the man, while my grandma asked him where he was from. I thought he was drunk because he was staggering, when he was actually hungry. He said he hadn't eaten in a couple of days, which made me feel twice as bad. My great grandma apologized for my behavior and sent him on his way. The kids followed him until he disappeared out of sight.

I think all of us kids in the neighborhood learned an important lesson. My great grandma told me to be careful, and to entertain strangers, because I may not know if I am entertaining an Angel. From that day on, I was a lot kinder to people who were a bit unfortunate. The same man returned on another day looking strong and robust. He found himself a job and he gave my great grandma some money and thanked her.

The school that I attended changed my attitude, which caused me stray from the basic principles that my grandma was trying to instill in me. When I reached the age of six, my mother came to the house and presented her case to my great grandma. I listened in on the conversation.

She said, "Sophia is getting older, and I want her to come and live with me."

"Why?" said my great grandma.

"Well, I want her to go to a good school where she can learn better. I don't want her going to the schools around here. I am going to get her into this Catholic school, it has a good reputation. Besides, her cousins go to the same school." she stated.

I did not want to leave my great grandma, but I was excited about the school.

She responded without protest, "Since you are going to get her into a good school, I have no choice. You can have her."

My mother did not waste any time. She packed up some of my clothes and we were on our way to her house. The house was spacious and spotless, she even had a refrigerator. Even though, I had everything a little girl could dream of, with all the fancy trimmings, I missed my great grandma. It wasn't long before I went back to live with her, but I continued to go to the new school.

The name of the school is Saint Jude's Primary. Every morning, all grades would meet for morning devotion in a secluded Hall, where we prayed and sing songs of praise. Every Thursday, all grades went to Mass. This was the only church I attended on a consistent basis. Isn't it ironic, I just realize that I did go to church. It was on a Thursday instead of a Sunday. I was praising God and I didn't know it. We use to all pray in unison at morning devotion. I thought it didn't count, even though I sang and prayed with all my heart.

I treasure those moments now, because most of the songs still plays a melody in my heart. This school had a good reputation for its academic excellence. Attending this school was like leading a dual life. At home I was shy and bashful and at school I was outgoing and popular.

My third grade teacher was not only a teacher, she was a socialite. In her class I develop a love for poetry and songs. Her style of teaching was a direct replica of her own life-style. She tried to instill pride, dignity and manners in us. In other words, she turned us into miniature snobs. She even despised reggae music.

The first big word I ever learned in school was "uncouth", which literally means to be ill mannered. I was taught how to use this word against my peers and my associates, if they did not behave accordingly. On occasion, I would use it, and find it quite funny, because the individuals did not know what it meant.

There is nothing wrong with learning about pride and dignity. The danger is we tend to use it as a weapon against others, who are less fortunate. We become critics, and try to force others to adhere to our superficial way of thinking. Usually, if anyone does not follow our behavior patterns, we place them in categories, and scorn them to shame. This is not a Biblical principle. I scorned a man who was literally hungry, because of false pride. Thank God my great grandma busted me down, big time.

In the fourth grade my behavior pattern continued. I could not stand the thought of someone being rude or ill mannered. One day I was with several of my friends talking, and one of my classmates came by us. He began to bother one of my friends, so she told him to leave her alone. He continued to interrupt our conversation and it was beginning to annoy me, so I broke my silence.

"Why don't you just get lost?" I scowled.

"Are you going to make me?" he replied.

I told him, "You have three chances to move away from here, and if you don't, I will make you move!"

He looked at me, and he looked at his friends and said in a mocking tone while he laughed. "Do you see the gal trying to test me?"

I warned him again, "This is your last warning. I am not playing, move or else..."

He dared me, "Else what!"

I boldly told him, "Or else I'll move you!"

He stood right in front of me and said, "You and what army!"

I simply pushed him away that he stumbled backwards. His eyes opened wide, he did not think that I would lay a hand on him. He charged forward. I waited until he came up close and pushed him down to the ground, but his pride would not let him stay down. He bounced back up again and attempted to charge again, but his friends held him back. They wrestled with him, but he was determined to come back, saying that he was not going to take it, so they let him go.

I waited until he charged again and pushed him further and further away. Out of the corners of my eyes, I saw my teacher walking in. My opponent did not see her, so he kept on charging and charging. She sat around her desk with her hands under her chin, waiting patiently with her head going back and fort.

The more I pushed him down, the more he got up saying; he was not going to take it. Finally, when my teacher thought that he's had enough, she clapped her hands twice, loudly.

"That's enough! Both of you get up here!" she yelled.

The both of us walked towards her and she asked us what happened, and I told her how it was started. We were both flogged with a flexible cane, and sent back to our seats. After that incident I acquired a reputation for being a no-nonsense type of person.

In my mind, I thought that I had all rights to physically stop someone from being rude, by using violence to solve the issue. Until I found out that I was exercising control over others. Even though it was not my intention, I was given a nickname, gained a great deal of respect and became very popular at school.

Secretly, I loathe the nickname they called me, even though I responded to it. They used it affectionately and did not mean any harm. Once, I heard them debating over the fact of who was the baddest person in school. The majority chose me. My pride was wounded. Deep down inside I was one of the biggest cowards. I was so sensitive that if an adult raised their voice at me I would literally cry. I wouldn't even open my mouth to defend myself in public, but I would defend anyone in a heartbeat.

There were two other classmates who were chosen, and they gave me this look of challenge. In their mind, I was a girl and how dare my classmates put me on top of the list. They were really bad, just for the sake of being bad. I was nervous at the thought of getting them upset at me. One of them went so far as to challenge me to a duel and the winner had to fight the remaining person. The winner of the final round would be declared the baddest person in the school.

Once again, others got involved, designating a place free from all teachers and adults. The first thing that entered my mind was the first fight I got into. How the fight was started, and why did I let it get out of control? I thought about how it could have been avoided, and how I lost the fight. My mind was made up quickly.

I boldly told everyone, "No! I do not want to fight anyone because someone could get hurt real bad."

To my surprise the crowd dispersed and I was respected for my decision. I would have lost; both guys had an advantage over me. They were wearing pants and I had on a skirt. Can you imagine the results? I probably would have had to change schools.

When I won the fight in the classroom, I was wearing a skirt. The difference is, I outsmarted my opponent, by letting him charge first, stood my ground and responded at the last minute.

I knew that I was cunning, quick and quite capable of beating anyone of my peers in the entire school. The fact of the matter is, if you know it you do not have to prove yourself to anyone. The greatest power anyone could have is to exercise the power of self-control.

The next time you find yourself in this position, "Think!"

Do you gain respect by beating someone who is weaker or not as cunning? They might do what you say, but secretly they hate your guts. There is a big difference between doing something out of respect and doing it out of intimidation. Not only are you pathetic, for trying to beat or put someone down to gain his or her respect. You lost all control, the moment you strike. The funny thing is you might end up in jail with someone as big as you are or even bigger, trying to gain your respect. Out of control, means you end up with no control.

My character began to change, becoming more empathetic towards my classmates. In the fourth grade, at ten years old, I was eligible to take an exam that would cause me to skip some grades and go straight to high school. My grandma would give me a double amount of money for lunch, because I was taking private lessons after school.

I would stay late playing after school and did not get home until after six, sometimes even later. At lunchtime, if I noticed anyone not eating lunch, secretly, I would buy him or her lunch. Free lunches were delivered to the various schools, but sometimes the truck did not show up.

I did not pass the exam, so I was forwarded to the fifth grade in a level one class. Before we broke for the summer, our teachers always allow us to meet with the teachers for the next school term. We formed a line and went to our designated classes. The teacher told us that we should show up for summer school everyday, with the exception of Fridays and the weekend. The classes were free, and it was going to cover the things that should be on the exam. The teacher also bragged that about two thirds of her class normally passes.

I went home and thought about it and did not want to ruin my summer vacation, so I stayed home. September came around and school started. On the first day we were given a math quiz. It was so easy. I finished, looked around, and everyone was still working. Therefore, I took it to one of the teachers.

"My! Are you finished already?" she said out loud.

"Yes," I replied, as my classmates looked up in amazement.

"Are you sure you don't want to take it back to your seat and re-check it again?" she remarked in a sly tone.

I said, "No," and walked back to my seat.

She corrected my paper and called me back and said real loud, "You have two wrong, you see if you had re-checked it, you would have had a hundred percent!"

She did it with a smirk, so that everyone in the class heard. I went back to my seat puzzled I thought I had it all correct, so I re-checked the answers. To my satisfaction, they were all correct. I turned to my classmate who had turned her work in and asked her to check it with me and we both thought they were correct. My classmate told me to go to the other teacher and have him correct it.

He did, and then shouted across the room to the other teacher, "You made a mistake! Sophia does have a hundred percent!"

"Oh! Let me see it, I guess you are right," she responded with a look of vengeance.

From that day on I was cautious of her. By the end of the week, we were given several quizzes. I passed every one, until we were given math problems that I did not recognize. This time, I was one of the last to hand my work in. I went up and I had five wrong. She told me to do the wrong ones over, and I told her that I did not know how to do it.

"So! Little miss perfect don't know how to do these math test, because she did not show up for summer school. You know what! Pack your bag, you are going next door to the lower level class!" She snarled.

My heart sank so low, I don't know what stopped me from bursting out into tears. Apparently, she wanted to get back at those who did not attend the summer classes.

My other teacher quickly pointed out, "Sophia is not the only one that does not know how to do those math problems, he doesn't know and she doesn't know how to do it either."

"O.K., all three of you, pack your bags now! You are going next door!" she shouted.

My bag was packed and I watched as my other two class-mates cried, begged and pleaded with her. I was the only one who did not respond, so she called me with her index finger. I responded, so she personally escorted me to the lower level class. I was devastated but I kept my dignity. When I was settled and given an assigned seat. I fought very hard to hold back the tears and never allowed them to roll down my cheeks. Eventually, I got over it.

The books that we had never showed us how to solve the math problems, they just presented the math problems. If someone did not show me how to solve them, I was basically clueless. It was a huge price to pay for not showing up for summer school. I had the opportunity to get a scholarship and graduate a year early with my best friend, but I chose the easy way out and was penalized greatly.

I hid the fact that I was set back to a lower level class and never discussed it at home. At home, I had the love and admiration from both adults and peers. I was always in a level one class. They thought that I talked, walked and carried myself in a dignified manner.

The sixth grade was the final grade of the school, and I finally made it back to a level one class. One day, our teacher gathered us together and told us she was going for an interview, to become the new Six O'clock Newswoman on the television. We were all excited for her, because she was a Saint Jude's alumni. She told us that if she gets the job, she would have to leave the class early everyday. Therefore, she asked us to elect someone in the class to represent her when she was not there. We were told to nominate several people.

To my surprise, my name was the first to be nominated. The other names were placed on the board also. I thought it was getting more competitive; someone just elected the prettiest girl in the class.

She stood up and said, "I decline."

We all looked at each other puzzled, until our teacher define the word for us. Then, she warned us not to choose anyone because of their looks. She wanted us to narrow the candidates down to five. We all voted and out of the five nominees, I received the most votes. I was so surprised. It was almost lunchtime, so our teacher told us to make our selection when we return.

During the lunch hour, I campaigned hard, not taking for granted that I had the most votes. The school bell rang and class resumed. Our teacher told all the nominees to go outside of the classroom. We all went outside and stood under this big shady tree, discussing who we think would win. They all said that I would win, but I never got my hopes up, anything could happen. Finally, our teacher called us in, and I won the most votes.

The teacher called me up in the front of the class. She stood by my side and said, "Sophia will represent me, whenever I am not here. I want you to respect her as you do me. Whatever she says goes, and no talking back to her. If I arrive the next day and I hear that anyone disrespects her, you are going to have to deal with me. Is that clear?"

The class said, "Yes."

Are there any questions?"

The class said, "No."

I held my head down, trying not to look at anyone in the classroom, I felt a little embarrassed. The next day our teacher arrived, and told us that she was going to be the new replacement on the Six O'clock News. Most of us jumped up and cheered. We were all excited for her.

It was time for her to leave early, so she called me up to sit around her desk and told me what is expected of me. I was still being bashful until she left. I stood up and warned them that I was told if anyone talks, I should write their names down. I sat back down and looked at all my classmates. I have never viewed them from this angle before. I felt power and prestige.

If my friends talked I would not write their names down or I would give them a second chance. If they were not in my circle of friends, I treated them differently. Once, I caught a classmate talking so I walked towards his desk to confront him. I spotted a mango on top of his desk, as he begged me not to tell on him. Therefore, I told him to give me his mango and I would not tell on him. He told me he could not give me the one he had, but he would bring me one the next day, so I did not write his name down. I would allow my friends to go to the bathroom and did not allow others to go.

One day, as class was about to begin, my teacher said, "I heard that Sophia was being unfair, using blackmail, and parading around as if she was high and mighty."

The classroom echoed with intervals of, "Yea!"

I was shocked, because the same people who I did not tell on, was agreeing with the teacher.

I said surprisingly, "Blackmail!"

"Did you or did you not ask one of your classmate for his mango or else you would tell on him?" She asked.

I just shut my mouth and listened to my accusers. After all, they did have a legitimate claim. She called me up in front of the class and told me to hold out my hands. This means that I am about to get flogged with a flexible cane.

With each strike she said, "When I left you in charge, I wanted you to be fair. You should not have let the position go to your head. And by the way, Blackmail is a punishable crime. You are fired! Get back to your seat!" she shouted.

Again, I was publicly humiliated. I went back to my seat, placed my head on my desk and cried. At lunchtime, I tried to find out who told on me. My head was so much into the clouds that I was blinded. I forgot that the teacher's niece was in our class.

One of my friends said to me, "Your classmates trusted in you, that is why they voted for you and you let them down."

Getting flogged, fired and publicly humiliated hurt, but the pain was more excruciating, at the thought of betraying the trust of my classmates.

The Bible said, "It is better to trust in the Lord than to put confidence in man." (Psalms 118:8) KJV

If you place all your trust in man, you are in big trouble. That is why people get easily hurt. They put all their trust in people, other than God. Do not put all your trust in your peers, men and women of the cloth, associates, teachers, family, friends, doctors, your lawyers, your bank, your politician etc.

Trust no one but God. Man is weak and is more likely to betray your trust. That is why you should pray over your food, your parents, your siblings, your relatives, your doctors, your lawyer etc. Pray that they will take on the characteristics of God.

We all have good intentions, until power and greed seduces us and take us under its spell. Some will sell their firstborn, lie, cheat, steal or use you to get ahead. We cannot even trust in ourselves. How many times have you said you were not going to do something and did it anyway? That is why we need to pray that God will lead, guide and direct our paths. We do not know what we will do, if a certain opportunity is given to us.

This reminds me of the misconceptions that people have, of how a Christian should conduct themselves. They think that once you walk down the aisles and give yourself to Christ. You should automatically become this perfect person. They watch your every move, expecting you to become this ideal role model. You have to dress a certain way, talk a certain way, walk a certain way and look a certain way. All eyes are on you until the moment you shatter their idealism of how a Christian should live. They blame the religion and God.

Don't be surprised if you see me belting out an old tune at a karaoke machine, dancing or making a complete spectacle of myself.

Then you make that dreaded remark that I come to loathe, "Aren't you a Christian?"

Jesus is my role model. I am not your role model. Don't put me on a pedestal. God sent Jesus to represent us as a role model, yet we view each other as role models. Christ will not disappoint you, but us Christians will. You inhibit us from being our selves. Therefore, we hide behind closed doors, and do the things you think we are not capable of doing.

CHAPTER FOUR

NECESSARY BACKSLIDE

I moved to the United States when I was thirteen years old, to live with my mother. Finally, I was in the land I heard so much about. For the second time in my life I was separated from my great grandma. Once the fascination wore off and reality set in. I realized that I may never see my granny again. She was no where close and I could not change my mind. There was no route of escape, as I did in the pass. I could not walk back home or hop on a bus. Panic set in and I would cry myself to sleep.

My mom would ask me what was wrong and I told her that I wanted to go back to Jamaica. She told me that she could not send me back. It did not help at all so I continued to cry every night.

One day she sat me down and said, "If you want, I will buy you a ticket to England so you could live with your grandma?"

"I don't want to go to England; I want to go back to Jamaica!" I protested.

"You don't have that choice. I cannot send you back to Jamaica. Do you want to go to England or stay here?" she asked.

I thought about it and she was right. I almost got killed running away from a political rally, where shots were fired. Then, the boys were beginning to notice me and it was my great grandma's wish. I was the one responsible for writing the letters to the various countries, while my granny dictated to me.

I remembered in one of the letters, she told me to write, "Please hurry and send for your daughter. It is getting worse out here!"

Once I hit puberty, it was as if Granny was in a panic mode. She was overly protective and watched my every move. I could have definitely ended up being a statistic. I eventually told my mother that I would stay. Once I made up my mind to stay, I stop crying myself to sleep.

I started going to church with my mom on a regular basis. My mom loved to dress up, so she turned me into a miniature dresser. The clothes I wore, were the choice of my mom. If I had a choice, I would wear something plain. I would go to Sunday school and then we assembled in church.

Since I was new to this country, I regressed back into my shyness, and did not want to leave my mother's side. Each Sunday the Pastor would give an invitation to join the church. My mom would try to push me to join the church, and I hated it, because I thought I was being forced.

Determined not to join the church until I felt something, I ignored her and stood my ground. One Sunday the invitation was given again, and I did not feel anything, so I ignored it.

Another adult who was sitting in front of me turned around and lowered her face in front of mine and said, "Aren't you going to go up and join the church?"

"I'm not ready as yet," I replied.

She leaned her face towards me and said, "You come in here with your fancy clothes, and you don't talk to nobody, thinking that you are better than everyone else. But I am here to tell you missy that you are no better than anyone else in here. You hear me, no one in this place!"

I was totally devastated. I did not join the church so she went after my pride. I wanted to let her know, that I was the one with the complex. I was just shy, home sick and heartbroken. Further more, I did not feel comfortable in the clothes that I was wearing.

It angered me, I was determined that I was not going to join the church unless I felt something.

One Sunday, Little Richard was the guess preacher. He talked about his real life drama, and what lead him to God. His testimony touched me, he talked about his past and how he found his way. I was drawn to the altar. Finally, I felt something.

Eventually, I joined the church and got baptized, but I still had bitter feelings towards the statement made, so I refused to go to church anymore. The lady stereotyped me, so I formed my own opinions of Christians. I thought they were cruel and mean. Since I pride myself on not being a phony, I did not want to associate myself with Christians. My mom thought I was a heathen.

Almost two years later, we moved to the suburbs, so I changed high schools. It was totally different from the schools in the city. They act, walked and talked differently, but I was determined to be myself no matter what.

My mother was a single parent with a mortgage to pay. She was advised that I could receive free lunches; by filling out a form they placed in my transfer packet. When school started in September, she filled out the form, and told me to give it to the proper personnel. I ripped up the form and continued to ask for lunch money.

"What happened to the form I filled out?" she asked.

"That is embarrassing! I wouldn't be caught dead collecting welfare," I replied.

"That is not welfare! I pay taxes to the town," She urged.

"It is welfare! I am not going to turn in the form," I answered.

"O.K., since you don't want to turn in the form, why don't you make yourself a sandwich, add some stuff to it and take it to school," she answered.

"I'm in high school and they don't take their lunch to school, that's embarrassing!" I moaned.

"Fine, you have a choice, either you turn in the form or pack yourself some lunch, but I don't have any money to give you," she warned.

I was determined not to turn in the form or pack myself any lunch. Each day, I would skip eating breakfast and lunch. The only time I would eat was when I got home from school and sometimes later in the evenings. It depends on if I had soccer practice or a game. I played because I just love the game. Soon, I was so disciplined not eating food during the day that it did not faze me. Now, I realized that I was fasting.

Whenever, I watched the news on television, they portrayed Blacks as if they were welfare mongers. I resented that, and was determined not to fall into that category.

My grades in the city schools were average, below average and failures. In Jamaica, I took my studies seriously, because I had a great motivator. It was called a cane. If I did not do my homework, my skin would be fired up at school. Attending school here made me realize that if I did not do my homework, there were no consequences. I did not have a teacher putting the pressure on me or the fear of getting hit, so I didn't do my homework.

The school counselor told me if I fail anything else, I was in danger of repeating a grade or the possibility of going to summer school. Well, school was kind of interesting to me. If my teacher was not exciting and dynamic, with the capability of keeping me at the edge of my seat, I would simply tune myself out.

Finally, at the end of the semester I changed classes and got the type of teacher that kept me at the edge of my seat. It was my biology teacher. Ever since I was a child, I wanted to go into the medical field. As a matter of fact, I wanted to be a doctor. Being a realist, I knew that I was not going to accomplish that dream with the grades I had. After biology, I took anatomy and physiology, cells and tissues and marine biology for the love of it.

These classes fascinated me so much, that the theory of Evolution vs. Creationism turned my world upside down. I did not heed to my teacher's warning about not forgetting God's theory, because there are still some things that a scientist cannot explain. My belief in God changed. I thought that we had enough proof that we evolved or appeared by some biochemical accident. The theory that God made us, left a trace of doubt in my mind. The scientist in the books provided adequate proof, according to what I have read. I was totally confused.

One day, my composition teacher left an assignment with our substitute teacher, to have us write something creative. Previously, I had an unfinished poem. I simply did it over and passed it in. The next day my teacher returned and I said to her.

"Did you read my masterpiece?"

"Meet me after class and we will discuss it," she replied.

I met her after class and she told me that the content was excellent; I just have to re-write certain areas that she recommended. I re-write it and re-write it, until it was both to our satisfaction. Mrs. McCormick was so excited that it scared me. To me it was not a big deal. I gave her a puzzled look. This was the result.

CURIOUS MIND

Where am I?
Who made me?
Who am I?
Please don't forsake me.

Like a wondering child
With a curious mind,
My imagination ran wild,
But the visions are so hard to find.

I have millions of questions,
Asked but unanswered?
Is heaven our destination?
Can knowledge and truth be measured?

We live; we die
Grow young and old.
Another mother cries-
Someone took her baby's soul.

She asked me if I mind, if she submits it to the school papers. I told her no, she seemed to be more excited than I was. Soon, I forgot about the incident. Several weeks later, I arrived in school and notice my name and poetry on every bulletin board. I was shocked and felt embarrassed. Eventually, those feelings went away when my classmates told me that they saw it. They were all ranting and raving about the poem. I was a bit upset though, because they left the fourth verse off. That was the best part.

I think my composition teacher felt something in the poem. She responded by bringing in the video taped version of, "The Scopes Trial." She told us to watch it, take notes then write a composition. I have never seen or heard of this trial, yet I was told it was a true story. I watched with intense scrutiny, letting both sides present their argument about the teachings of Evolution verses Creationism.

Personally, I did not think that we evolved from apes, yet the belief that God created us was very confusing. Being the independent thinker that I was, I did not like being forced to believe in something without having proof. This caused me to choose a side very quickly. I did not accept the argument that we should dismiss the theory of evolution and replace it with the theory of the God.

Let me be clear, that neither side could prove their theory beyond a reasonable doubt. The difference is evolution used book sense and creationism used common sense. The side representing evolution, whose theory states that we evolved from apes, won the case. The other side representing creationism, whose theory states that we were created by God, lost the case.

They lost the case because they lacked knowledge, wisdom and understanding over the very subject they were trying to defend. The points presented were done out of anger and rage, giving the message that it was not about God the Creator. It was about man's ideal to impose their belief on others whether they like it or not. This was done without presenting their arguments with proper knowledge of the Bible. They did not have the book sense. Therefore, common knowledge was used in a forum that requires scientific data.

What was shocking to me was the thought that some of the observers were willing to commit violent acts, or kill if necessary all in the name of God's defense.

I thought to myself, "What kind of a God is this, who would want an individual to use violence or kill another because of their ideals?"

My mind was made up and this drove me away from God even further. I wrote my composition as honestly as I could without bias and turned it in. When I got my grade back it was a "C" I was upset but I know that I told the truth.

Then, I met the ultimate of teachers, who literally changed my life forever, Mrs. Laurie Costa. Her style of teaching was radical. It slapped me in the face, woke me up, and challenge me to look at myself, others and the world I live in. This kept me at the edge of my seat. With my curiosity, I wanted to learn more.

For the first time in my school history, I held my hand up on numerous occasions saying, "Could you repeat that please?"

The next semester, I saw that she was teaching a class on Human Rights. I quickly signed up, not knowing what I was getting myself into. This class was so powerful, it reshaped the way I viewed and looked at things. One of our first assignments was to choose a topic on stereotypes and do a report on it. There were plenty of topics on that subject, but I wanted mine to be an original.

I did not know what to choose, so I skipped through some old magazines my mom had. To my delight, I stumbled on an article that was entitled "Who Gets Welfare." I read through the article and was amazed. The way Blacks were portrayed on television, I thought they totally capitalized on welfare. This causes others to despise the race by using demeaning adjectives to describe the whole.

I was shocked to find out that Blacks were not the ones with the most welfare recipients. Secondly, welfare comes in various forms which include corporate, disability, housing, food stamps, social security, grants and others.

According to the statistics other races receive more benefits than Blacks. I took it to class and wrote the statistics on the board. I could tell that it was a stereotype that plagued this country which causes hate and resentment. I literally saw jaws dropped from the shock, even my teacher was surprised. She wanted a copy of the article.

Our next assignment was to document the plight of a certain group of people who had to suffer. Again, I searched for something original. I found another interesting fact, the plight of the American Indians. We are so caught up in our own causes that we forgot about a people who have sacrificed their home and country for the benefit of others.

Then, there were talks and negativity surrounding immigrants. The most ironic thing is the very people who are talking, their forefathers were once immigrants. They were not the originators of the land. Typical of some people, they want to benefit while others should be denied the rights to do so.

I learned so much in that class, but most of all I gained understanding, especially how easily one can be manipulated into buying, lying, stealing, killing and hatred. People with low self-esteem make excellent targets. Ignorance blinds the eyes of a fool, making them vulnerable to the evildoers. This includes cults, hate groups, and any religion that kills innocent people in the name of God.

Over the years, I've seen and heard the Bible taken out of context and most of the people are clueless, because they do not read it for themselves.

Soon, I started to take an interest in writing poetry, it came naturally to me. One day I showed my mom some of my writings.

She asked, "Did you write these?"

"Yes!"

"You're lying, you did not write these!" she sounded surprised.

"Oh yes I did!" I replied.

She responded, "You're lying, you copied it from the poetry book you had."

I went and got the poetry book and told her to let me know when she found the page I copied it from. She seemed shocked. I guess she could not believe that her big underachiever had such capabilities. My mom tried to talk to me about not doing my homework and my bad grades. I always told her not to worry about it.

We would watch Jeopardy and I would wipe out a whole category and more to prove to my mom, I was smart in my own way. One day, when the final question was asked, I laughed and said it was easy. According to the degree of difficulty, she bet that I would not get it right. I waited until the last second and blurted out the answer, and it was correct. She stood there silent, as I pranced around.

Finally, she responded, "You cannot achieve what you want to achieve, with those grades."

I stop bragging because she was right. I had to repeat my senior year. I failed typing, computer science and got low grades in anything that did not fascinate me. In the final two years of high school I made a conscious effort to improve my grades. My grades were improved but it was already too late, the damage was already done.

I took the SAT and hit an all time low I was forced to face reality. What college would want me with all my failures? My dreams of being in the medical field seemed out of reach? I felt basically doomed.

I completed high school and my future seemed unattainable. I could not get a regular job, not after I failed typing and computer science. It was suggested that I go to a community college. I looked through the brochure to choose an allied health profession that fit my requirements. Surgical Technician was my only choice. I did not know there was such a profession. It fascinated me, until I looked at the requirements. I had to have a "B" average and an SAT combination score of 900 or above, that eliminated me for sure. I looked at the prices to attend college and I was shocked, being ignorant about loans and grants.

I gave up on college and started to look for a job, and no one called. I felt as if I was surrounded by enemies, with no way out. I had no money, car, skills, family or friends. As usual, I try to handle things on my own without asking for help.

Finally, I could not take it anymore. I went to bed and cried from the bottom of my heart.

"My God, my God why have thou forsaken me," I groaned.

There I was crying to a God that I turned my back on. Pondering the thought that He did not made me, and thinking that He did not exist. Now, I was actually trying to blame God for my troubles. Then, I have the nerve to ask God for help.

"Why did you bring me to this country to be humiliated, talked about, made fun of, and most of all to fail?"

Actually, I could not remember the last time I had prayed. I was too busy learning the different man-made theories and speaking those big scientific words. If anything went wrong in my life, I blamed it on God. The more I blamed God, the more I separated myself from anything that pertains to God. Now, there I was on my hands and knees crying out to a God, I failed to acknowledge.

CHAPTER FIVE

THE MILITARY

After searching countless hours trying to find a job, I saw an interesting ad in the newspaper. The ad stated that if you wanted a job, call the number listed. I wanted a job, so I called the long distance number immediately. I called and left my name and number, only to find out it was the U.S. Navy. When I told my mom, she laughed and thought it was the funniest thing.

They returned my call and referred me to a local representative in my area. I thought about the possibilities of joining the Navy, but I could not swim. I did not want to be on a ship because I thought it was not lady-like. Then, I thought about the discipline, which made it even worst.

I analyze the situation and to be honest, I did not have a choice. A couple of days later, I called the local representative and went in for an interview. They asked me some questions, I filled out some paperwork, and then they weighed me. As if anything else could go wrong, I was 35 pounds overweight.

After high school I started to eat regular meals per day and more, which caused me to gain weight. They told me to loose 35 pounds then give them a call. There I was, it was my last hope and I had to loose 35 pounds. I don't know about you, but can you see a way out of my predicament. I was afraid to try anything, because I thought I would fail.

I went home and decided that I was going to loose those extra pounds and join the Navy. The recruiting officer was very supportive, as he would call on occasion to check on my progress. Since I had disciplined myself not to eat during the days in high school, I adopted the same techniques. It was very ironic. When I was in high school I did not care if I ate or not, now that I was dieting I felt the urge for food.

Eventually I lost 32 pounds, which was close enough. The next thing I know, I had a physical, some tests were taken and I was on my way to basic training. On one of the forms I filled out, it asked about my religious preference?

I thought about it and I wrote, "No religious preference."

The day before I left for basic training, my mom had a going away party for me.

"So! What are you going to do in the Navy?" asked one of the guess.

"They told me fireman apprentice," I answered.

My mother exclaimed, "Fireman what!"

"What do they do?" asked the same guess.

"I don't know, I guess they put out fires." I answered.

My mom seemed upset, but I did not care I decided to follow along blindly.

While we were in basic training, we were given telephone privileges, so I decided to call my eldest half sister who lived in another state. No one knew except for my mom where I was, so I thought she would be surprised.

"Guess where I'm at?" I asked.

She quickly responded, "Where?"

"I'm calling you from Boot Camp, I joined the Navy!"

Before I could say anything else, I heard her say to her husband in the back ground, "Honey, guess what! Sophia ran away from home and joined the Army."

I interrupted her and said, "I did not run away from home, and get it straight, I am in the Navy."

Our time was up so I had to get off the phone. I was a bit irritated, I thought I was grown enough to make my own decision. The next time we received our telephone privilege again, I called my dad.

Before I could get a word out of my mouth he said, "Oh my God Sophia! Your sister told me that you ran away from home and joined the Army. Tell me where you are and I will come and get you!"

"You cannot come and get me, I signed a contract. Furthermore I did not run away from home, and it is not the Army, it is the Navy. I joined it of my own free will."I said convincingly.

"Does your mom know about this?" He asked.

"Yes!" I declared.

"Oh! You know, you can still get out of that contract," he replied.

"Dad, I joined the Navy because I wanted to," I replied.

Finally, he gave up. When basic training was almost completed, I was sent to the career counselor. I went to her office wondering, what else is going to happen to me? I walked in the office and sat down.

She said, "Sophia, we were watching you and we don't think you would be happy being a fireman apprentice, do you?"

"No," I answered.

"How about bookkeeping or do you want a typing job?" She asked. She must have seen the horror on my face.

I said, "Typing! I failed typing in high school."

I realized what I had just said and thought, "Why did you say that Sophia, don't let anyone know that you failed anything."

I surprised myself. I did not want to say that.

She looked at me puzzled and said, "Well, what do you want then?"

"Do you have anything medical, because the only thing that I am good at is biology? I took human anatomy and physiology, cells and tissues and marine biology in high school," I stated.

"Well, as a matter of fact we have Corps School, which is like a nurses' aid," she stated.

I patiently waited as she looked through her papers.

She looked up, smiled and said, "Great! We are looking for people just like you and we have a spot."

I was so happy I could do cart wheels. She informed me more about the school and told me I can go immediately after basic training. I shook her hand and accepted the school.

Finally, I graduated from Boot Camp. I thought I was not going to make it, and then took a flight immediately to Corps School. When I arrived, I stitched on the medical insignia on the sleeve of my shirt. I was at the lowest rank but I was proud. Soon, I got situated and classes began.

Midway through Corps school, we were given a choice to request a more advanced school. We had to choose the schools according to our rank. The lower your rank, the lesser your choices were. In high school I got an "A" in psychology, so I requested something in the psychological field. One of my instructors came up to me and advised me not to choose anything based on my rank. She told me I could end up getting something that I did not like, so I requested nothing.

Failure plagued me again. I almost failed demonstrating certain skills. I had to fight myself to make what I read applicable. I had book sense, but lacking in the commonsense department. The classes were condensed, so there was no time for our instructors to baby us. We were given packets to read on our own, and had to demonstrate these skills.

I read the packet and went to class the next day. My instructor called me out of the group, and asked me to show the class what I had learned. I knelt beside the dummy and did not know where to begin. There I was, with all eyes on me and I was dumbfounded. One of the instructors tried to help, by asking me a series of questions. It only proved that I was clueless. The instructor got upset and made an example out of me. I felt embarrassed.

We went back to our living quarters and I spoke to one of the young ladies, a class ahead of me and told her what happened. She felt bad for me and tried to teach me the routine. It was as if I was being thought from her point of view. I only got bits and pieces of the information. This motivated me to want to read it, comprehend it and demonstrate it for myself. I stayed up practically all night reading and talking to myself, pretending as if my pillow was the dummy.

The next time my instructor singled me out, I knelt beside the dummy and demonstrated the necessary skills with confidence. Then, I was asked a series of questions, and was given different types of scenarios. I thought about it, and I was able to answer them based on the packet I had read. You should have seen the look on my instructor's face, he was shocked.

This was my first path to gaining commonsense. I realized that I have to make myself accountable for acquiring essential knowledge, by not relying on others. You only get some of the facts. I have to read all information available, for myself.

Corps school was coming to an end, and our orders came in. I looked at mine and liked the place I was going to, but I noticed that I had an advance school to attend. It was listed as O.R. School. This was strange, I did not request a school, yet I received one and did not know what it was.

I raised my hand and asked, "What is O.R. school?"

One of my classmates said, "Hey! That's my orders. I requested that school."

We had the same last name, so I thought it was a mistake. Our instructor told us that O.R. school is an Operating Room Technician who worked in all aspects of the operating room. Then, she told us she would investigate the orders. My heart sank; I knew it was too good to be true. To request that school, you had to be a certain rank and I was at the lowest rank.

After several days of uncertainty, the other Jones and I were called to the instructor's office. We were told to have a seat. Thinking it was a hint that one of us is going to be disappointed. I braced myself for the rejection.

Her eyes looked at the both of us individually, while she said, "I went to investigate your orders and I fought hard for the both of you, but..."

The other Jones leaned forward intently, while I slouched back slowly.

She continued, "I had a long talk with them and guess what?"

My head hung low and ceases to have eye contact. The other Jones looked as if she dared the instructor to tell her, she didn't get it.

She smiled and said, "You both are going!"

We were all relieved and happy. As soon as Corps School was over, I took a short vacation. Then, I was on another flight again to my next duty station. I was very happy, had lots of friends and was living like a brat. Soon, I forgot about the fact that almost a year ago I was surrounded by uncertainty. Now, I could see where I was going. I even forgot about crying out to God, because I did not have anywhere else to turn. Now, I was busy enjoying my newfound freedom. I thought it was luck.

Joining the Navy was one of the best things that happened in my life. It was as if someone took me by the hand, and gave me a first class tour of what real life was all about. I had a self-righteous mental attitude. I did not drink, smoke, do drugs, been to clubs, or socialized much with others. I lived a sheltered life and avoided people who drank, smoke or did anything I thought was bad.

My other aspiration was to go into politics, so all I cared about was my self-image. Standards were set and I wanted to adhere to them. Then again, if I had a choice I would isolate myself from everyone. I had a love hate relationship with my fellow man. Sometimes I despise them for the way they treat each other, yet I felt empathy for its victims.

Sometimes we think that we are the only one that bad things happen to, but think again. Being exposed to people of different races and cultures, uncovered the plight of human beings.

The general question asked by almost everyone is, "Why did you join the military?"

I would sit and listen to the various responses. The more I heard, the more I realize that we all go through the same things. You might think you have the ultimate problem, until you hear the story of another. Some of the stories were so heartbreaking that when you look back at your life, your problem is minor.

In my stereotypical mind, I thought that Whites had it very easy in life, because of the color of their skin. Think again, their stories were the ones with the most heartbreak. We all have a story to tell, no one is immune.

It was New Year's Eve night, and a group of us from the barracks went down town to get some frozen yogurt. When we arrived, I saw some balloons stuck to the ceiling. Being in a playful mood I asked the cashier if I could have some balloons, she gave me two. We ate our yogurts and soon we were on our way. We were walking down the street laughing, joking, and having fun, with my balloons tied around my wrist.

I looked down and saw a homeless man lying on the sidewalk. It was chilly and he was exposed to the cold air. I could not laugh anymore, I thought here I am laughing, joking and having fun and there is this person, with no one who cares for him. He was out cold, but I know enough that he was not dead.

I pulled out some money, tucked it in his hands and said, "Happy New Year."

The poor man was out, sleeping his cares away. My friends saw this and they all had their own opinions.

"You shouldn't give them any money because someone may beat him up and take away the money," said one.

"You shouldn't give him any money, because you are only encouraging him to stay on the streets," said another.

"I wouldn't give them any money period. I hardly have enough money to take care of myself," said another.

"He's only going to take it and buy alcohol," said another.

I responded, "Even if he takes it and buy alcohol, it would keep him warm, at lest I try to do something about the situation."

They were all silent for a while until we got back on base. I could not understand why people felt this way. We have all lost our compassion, but I continued to give.

I remember my grandma would tell us, "Give and the Lord will give you more."

Another time, my best friend came to visit me and was in danger of missing her flight. We went across the border to do some last minute shopping and got back late. We had to get back on base immediately, but could not find a bus or taxi to take us, so we began to walk. As we were about to cross over a major street, we saw two homeless people in the middle of traffic, trying to stop the moving cars.

I thought to myself, "Are they crazy, they are going to get hit!"

The cars zoomed pass them, ignoring their plight. One of them turned around to see us waiting to cross the street and asked if we could spare some money for some food. I went into my pocket and pulled out a twenty dollar bill and gave it to the woman. She waved it in the air and told the other to look at what she got. He hurried towards us with his bright red face, baked from an overdose of sun.

Soon my eyes opened wide, as the woman came towards me with open arms. She had on several layers of clothing that looked like dirty rags.

I thought to myself, "She is not going to hug me is she, oh no!"

She gave me a big hug, kissed me on the cheek and said, "Thank you!"

The other man seemed shocked. He told us that they have been out there for a very long time and no one stopped to give them anything and they were hungry. I was in a hurry, so I told them I had to go and to be careful not get hit by a car.

"God bless you!" the woman shouted.

I told her, "Thanks!" as my best friend and I waved.

Of all the times, there were taxi cabs begging for us to use their services, and they were no where to be found.

I graduated from, O.R. school and was on my way back to the East coast, closer to home. One weekend I visited my mom and she invited me to church. I always try to get out of going to church. It was six years since I last went. I always say that Christians were a bunch of hypocrites. I told my mom I could not make it, because I did not have a dress with me.

Purposely, I did not pack a dress so I could have an excuse, not to go to church. My mom went right into her closet and found a dress that fits me perfectly.

It was weird being back in church, the place where I once loved. To make matters worst the pastor preached about tithing.

I said to myself, "Great! The day I decided to go to church in a long time and the pastor decided to talk about money."

"Can I get a witness?" said the pastor.

My mom jumped straight up, put her hands in the air and said, "Yea!" real loud.

I was the type of person that gets embarrassed easily.

I thought, "Is this really my mom! I hope she sits down before she embarrasses herself."

She sat down, and I breathe a sigh of relief. We continued to listen and the pastor asked again, if he could get a witness. My mom jumped up again, without a care in this world. I was so shocked. I thought my mom was an impostor. My mom was very shy, ladylike and prissy, all dressed up in her fancy clothes and heels. She was very reluctant to raise her hands for anything publicly.

On our way back home, I was thinking how to approach my mom without embarrassing her. I was still in disbelief about what I heard and saw. As soon as we got in the house I approached her gently.

"What happened to you? The pastor is talking about giving ten percent of your pay check and you are excited."

My mom is single with a mortgage to pay on one salary. I was very curious; I thought she had hit the jackpot.

She proclaimed, "When it comes to being a witness for God, I am not ashamed. Whenever I receive my paycheck, I made sure I gave my ten percent."

I exclaimed, "Ten percent!"

She nods her head and said, "Sometimes I did not know how I was going to pay the mortgage. But because I believe and trust in God, He made a way."

On the flight back I thought to myself, there is a presence out there. I could not deny the fact that there is a God and

I could not tell anyone that there is a God. I could not take someone else's word. I had to know God for myself. I had peace, joy, compassion, and knew the difference between right and wrong, but God, I did not know.

CHAPTER SIX

DISCHARGED

In 1991 I received an honorable discharge from the Navy, so I took a month off trip to Jamaica. It had been ten years, since I went back to visit, I longed to see everyone. I was hoping to see my great grandma, before anything happen to her. I loved and admired that woman so much that I would give my life for her.

There were so many questions that I wanted to ask her. She was a preacher's daughter and was spiritually gifted. I had brief memories of things I had witness as a child and was very confused.

I was told that she almost died twice, and came out acting as if she saw an uncle of mine that died.

She was calling out his name saying, "There he is! There he is!"

My curiosity was at its peak, and I wanted to ask her what she saw. Finally, the plane was grounded and my heart skipped a beat. As I walked down the stairs of the plane, the hot air hit me and I felt joy. I could not believe that I made it.

My uncle, aunt and cousin were there to meet me. They drove me home and the place looked smaller than I remembered as a child. My heart beat faster as I entered the house in search of my great grandma. My uncle went ahead of me and announced to her that I was finally here. She jumped up, called out my name with open arms, as I hurried to greet her. The hugs seemed like an eternity, it was late at night so we all went to bed.

I woke up early the next morning, and went out side to see how things have changed. I could not believe that I remembered almost everyone's face and name. They were more surprised than I was. Each day, the house became more hectic, it was always filled with visitors.

My uncle lived in a fancy apartment uptown St. Andrew and told me I could stay there. I told him that I rather stay with my great grandma. Where we lived at, was at the bottom of Trench Town. I couldn't wait to spend some quality time with my grandma.

Three of my uncle's children and granddaughter came to visit. I express to them my feelings, to go and visit my father's mother and relatives. I was warned not to walk through the area; for fear that something might happen to me. I simply shrug it off and took my cousins with me. Then, I traced my tracks where I use to go when I visited as a child.

We walked through water logged roads, slums and ghettos of Trench Town without a care in this world. Then my cousins dared me to go to Rema, a political hot spot. Even I know from before I left Jamaica that many died there from gun shot wounds. They thought I was too good, to walk in certain areas and I prove them wrong. We were almost home, when I turned the corner to see my uncle's car, he seemed worried and in a panic mode.

He said, "Do not take it for granted walking through these areas, you could get killed!"

"Don't worry, I'll be all right," I answered.

My great grandma reprimanded me also. They thought I was still that shy, timid girl that left the island.

My eldest cousin took me aside and said, "I like your attitude, most people when they return for visits, they stay in some fancy hotel. Most of them are afraid to visit their families. If they do, they usually end up showing off in front of their friends and family."

"Really! That's too bad. I am a plain ordinary person and I do not see the need or necessity to impress anyone." I remarked.

Most people when they go back to visit, they put on extra jewelry, fancy clothes and shoes to impress others. This is a terrible plight. They give the impression as if the streets in America are paved with gold.

My cousins invited me to their house situated in a nice area. Then, the one that told me that he liked my style took me through some more waterlogged streets, slums and ghettos to meet his baby boy. I told him I wanted to meet everyone, who is a part of the family. He felt comfortable around me, so we let our guards down. After all our visits, we went back to their house and they wanted me to stay, but I could not. I had a granny to interrogate.

After getting use to the weather, and meeting almost everyone, finally, I get to spend some time with my granny. Laying my head in her lap, I told her about the countless dreams of this moment to see her again. The questions that I wanted to ask her, popped up.

"They told me that you almost died twice, do you remember anything?"

She gave me this strange look and said, "Yes," hesitantly.

"Could you tell me what happened?" I probed.

"What do you want to know that for?" She said curiously.

"I have to know for myself, if there is a God and where do we go when we die?" I replied.

"Well! I can tell you this; there is a Heaven and a Hell..."

"How do you know that?" I interrupted.

"Because I saw it, I was walking on top of these long pegs and I looked down and saw a pit with a lot of people down there. Then, I saw the devil and he was pouring this big cast iron pot of hot water on the people. They were crying out in misery, and as some of them tried to climb out of the pit, he burnt them with fire sticks and they fell back into the pit. The sides were lined with grease, so they could not escape. They were climbing on top of one another to get out, they would either slide back down or they get burnt with the fire sticks, she explained in horror."

"And what else did you see?"

"Well, I held my head straight and walked on the pegs until I saw a different place, as I walked down from off of the pegs...."

"What did it look like?" I interrupted.

"It looked peaceful and green, then I saw mammy and pappy and my little daughter that died and...."

"Did you see God?" I interrupted again.

"No!" she replied.

I tried to ask her more questions but she seemed irritated, so I did not ask any more questions.

The next day I asked her about her gift of healing. She did not mind talking about that, she talked on and on about all the people she had helped. She also pointed out that, usually these people came to her as a last resort, when everything else failed.

"And it worked?" I asked.

"Yes! With the exception of this one man. He was a nice looking handsome fellow, but his head was turned to the side and his mouth was twisted. They brought him to me and his head straightened up and his mouth was not twisted anymore. He was even better looking. I gave him specific instructions and told him to be careful but he ended up being a wild man, with lots of women. Before you know it, his head and mouth went back the same way because he did not listen." She replied.

"How did you, heal those people?" I asked.

"I pray and ask God and it is revealed to me, what plants to pick and what to do."

"Do you remember the plants?" I asked.

She listed off some names and I tried to write them down, but whom was I kidding. As if I was going to go in the bushes of Jamaica to pick anything that I do not know about. Then something went off in my head.

"Can you come up with a cure for cancer, because if you do we could become millionaires?" I exclaimed.

As soon as I mentioned money, all the questions and answers were stopped. It was the way she looked at me.

My great grandma was one of the most sincere, compassionate, kind and honest person I have ever known. When I was an infant, my mom wanted to move out of the house and take me with her. My grandma told her that if she took me away, she was going to sue her. I did not find this out until later, apparently she won the battle.

Why she favored me, I do not know. Some observers told me that when I was a baby, she was so protective of me, that no one could touch me. As a child growing up, her preferential treatment was so obvious that everyone around us was aware of it. Little did they know that if I was caught doing anything wrong, I was reprimanded intensely and immediately.

She was well respected, and knew people in high and low places even though she was not rich. With the gift she had, she could have made a lot of money. Most of what she did was done in private or was done on a charitable basis. My childhood days were spent by her side, she was simply amazing. After she cooked and we ate, she would take me all over by foot visiting friends, especially those who were sick.

By the time we got home, we had a handful of things. People would give her money, food, and more without her asking them. On our way home, she would give most of it away to others. I use to think, why is she giving away the stuff? Then, I realized that the more she gave the more she received.

In the seventies there was an embargo forced on Jamaica. Cuba was interfering and getting involved in our country. The embargo caused the prices of everything to go up and food was getting scarce. You couldn't get certain items and we were beginning to feel the pinch. My granny prayed and the next day this man showed up on his bicycle with a huge box on his handle bar, in front of our gate.

As my great grandma went out to greet him, she held her hands up and praised the Lord. It was the baker my grandma would buy special bread from. We did not have a telephone, so she did not call him. It was my first time meeting him. He pulled out a loaf of bread, gave it to her and asked her if she knew anyone who wanted to buy bread. Some of the neighbors bought bread but others could not afford it, so he gave it to them on credit. The baker then handed the responsibility over to my granny. She would then collect the money and take orders for more bread.

Soon, certain items were being rationed. If you wanted to purchase a bottle of cooking oil, you had to purchase two or three other items with it, even though you did not intend on it. They used the term that all the items grouped together for sale, were married. Most of the time you end up getting unwanted items or spending more money than you bargained for.

One day, one of the neighbors sent his daughter to invite my granny over to his house. She took me along with her. He gave her a five pound bag of flour, placed in a dark bag to hide its contents. He told her that he worked at the flour mill, and had some extra bags and he thought about her.

She could have kept her mouth shut, taken the bag home, and cared not for others. Instead, she spoke up and made a bargain with him, to sell some of the flour to the neighbors who could afford it and gave it to those who could not afford it on credit. Again, she would make sure that things were distributed to the families in need. Then, she collected the money and took orders for more flour.

She was not working at the time and there were no retirement benefits; neither was she operating in her gifts. She kept complaining that she could not see anymore, yet I pointed out to my other relatives that she could read the newspaper. When I finish reading the newspaper she bought for me, we would sit and converse about some of its contents. She was in her seventies at the time.

Now that I know what I know, she either had cataracts or she could not see in the spiritual realm.

My Grandma Racheal, lived in England, who is my granny's daughter. She would send us money and care packages filled with clothes and food. Instead of my granny keeping things for us only, she would share it with the neighbors. When the neighbors get anything, they would share it with us also. That was how we survived that era. I never went to bed hungry, but I had to do without other material things. Then, I left for the States.

The next several days while visiting Jamaica, I would tease her.

"Have you come up with the cure for cancer as yet? We could be millionaires." I joked.

She would just turn her face from me, without saying anything. The week passed by and it was Sunday. I woke up to hear someone preaching on the television, so I got dressed quickly and went to take a look and saw a Jamaican Television Evangelist.

"You guys have one of them too!" I exclaimed.

I was not a great fan of television preachers, so I started to express my opinions, on what I thought of them. Apparently, I was heard by my great grandma. She whipped the curtains to the side and busted from around the corner, with a cross look on her face, as she looked at me directly.

"You can stay there and think that there is no God. You are very fortunate. If God was like man! All you care about is money!" she snarled.

I sat there silent for a while and was very hurt. I wanted to tell her that I really didn't care about money and I'm not a materialistic person. After all, she was the one who raised me to be the person that I am and I did not want to disappoint her. The same thing she was accusing me of, was the same thing I was accusing the television preacher of.

I had to seriously think about it; there I was asking her to figure out a cure for cancer using God, saying we could be millionaires. Yet, the preacher asks for money to do God's work. I was no different than the very thing I was against.

My grandma sure had a way of making me humble myself. The conversations that I had with her from that day on were far different than before. Now, I was more sensitive to the needs of my grandma, I only asked her questions about her hopes, wishes, health and family background. I forgot that her father was the pastor of a church and she was also called by God.

I began to realize that I was not the same Sophie to her. As I matured I developed this warped sense of humor that is dry and somewhat questionable. If you do not know me personally, you would find it offensive or try to take it personally.

One day, I was awoken by loud cries and mumbling words. I put on my robe, went outside and looked around to find out what household it was coming from. I located the area and saw whom it was coming from. There was no one hurting her, yet she was crying out and saying that why doesn't someone specific do something. I went back into the house and my grandma asked me who it was, and I told her.

We both try to ignore the noise. The next day the same thing happened, so I asked a friend of mine, what was wrong with her? He told me that she does it through certain periods of time. The next day again, the same thing, I was really getting annoyed. Another thought came to me, as I looked at my grandma.

"Can you look at her and fix her please?" I asked.

She shrugged me off, I insisted, so she finally told me to send for her. The lady came to our house crying and making accusations saying, "Why won't people do the right thing? She won't do certain things when she should be doing certain things."

She went on and on referring to someone specific.

My grandma finally said sternly, "Why are you picking up other people's burden?"

"But...." She started.

"Stop worrying about other people, worry about your-self," interrupted grandma.

I was told to read a certain scripture while my grandma prayed for her and send her on her way with specified instructions. Soon, I forgot about the whole incident, the days were too hot to think. The next day my grandma brought it to my attention.

"You see! She stop crying out," she said.

I went outside and listened, I heard nothing. For the following weeks that I was there I did not hear any crying or loud screams again. I was simply amazed.

Soon my vacation was over and I came back to the States. I could not wait to tell a couple of my mom's friends what had happened. They were always trying to get me to attend church. I usually tell people that I need to find the Lord for myself, because I would be faking it if I go to church.

I finally saw my mom's friends again and couldn't wait to tell them what happened. They asked me about my trip, and I told them about my experience with my grandma.

One of them said to me, "Can I be honest with you?"

I braced myself and said, "Yes."

"I am sorry to say this, but that is witchcraft and your grandma is going to go to hell," she snarled.

I was very hurt, but I maintained my composure. Those were some strong words.

"She is a pastor's daughter; she prays almost everyday and she is one of the kindest people I have ever met!" I proclaimed.

She exclaimed, "It doesn't matter, she is going to hell!"

We changed the subject, I was upset but I did not let it show. I had taken a few steps forward towards God, but at that time I took several steps back.

I said to myself, "I do not want to serve a God, who would destroy someone with the integrity of my great grandma."

This is the perfect example of how we let others turn us off of God. Three years later my great grandma passed away and I returned to Jamaica to attend the funeral. I was living in another state at the time. My mom arrived before I did and met me at the airport. The next day we greeted the neighbors as they gave us their condolences.

I saw the lady that was crying out when I visited three years ago. She remembered when my great grandma and I prayed and helped her out. She told us how good God have been to her and how wonderful He is. I could not talk to her because I did not know what she felt, so I referred her to my mom.

I still did not attend church, pray or read my Bible. I was happy for her; she now reads her Bible and attends church on a regular basis.

I thought, "This lady has surrendered her life to God. How could my great grandma do witchcraft and the results were positive?"

"But Jesus knew their thoughts, and said unto them, Every kingdom divided against itself is bought to desolation; and every city or house divided against itself shall not stand: And if Satan cast out Satan, he is divided against himself; how shall then his kingdom stand?" (Matthew 12:25, 26) KJV

If I had a great army and my objection is to conquer the world. First, I would have to come up with a strategy. To obtain my goal, I would have to form an alliance with several countries. Say, we signed a deal stating that for every country captured, the spoils would be divided equally.

Being greedy, I went back on the deal. After all, it was my idea so I think I deserve most of the spoils. Therefore, I made a decision to attack the countries that my alliances are occupying. Why would I plan such a strategy? This would definitely ruin my objective.

Pretend that your body is the country being occupied and you sent out a distress signal. A powerful and mighty nation heard your distress and sends some help for you. They came and heal you of your ailment and drive the enemy out.

Why would you accuse the help of working for the enemy? Do you think the enemy would send someone to help you? Thank God for his gifts and my great grandma. I have no doubt of her final resting place.

CHAPTER SEVEN

MY BEST FRIEND

My best friend and I are two opposite people, yet we share a basic humanity towards our fellowman. I have to give credit where it is due, my best friend is an integral part of my life, which forced me to stop being an observer and join the human race. We met in Corps school in the Navy.

One night while I was in the barracks, I heard someone asking for a volunteer to escort someone on a jog. I looked at my watch and saw that it was close to midnight.

I thought, "Who in their right frame of mind would want to go for a jog, at this time of the night."

I got out of bed to investigate and saw this young lady whom I have never seen before insisting that she had to go out for a jog. Still, there were no volunteers. I did not want to jog so I tried to change her mind, by making her aware of the dangers.

"You could get raped out there at this time of the night," I said.

"I'll be fine! If no one wants to go, I'm going anyway," she replied.

We could not stop her, so I volunteered. We started to jog and she struck up a conversation. I wish she didn't because I was out of shape and gasping for every air I breathe. I could hardly respond to her. It was bad enough that I had to keep up with her, now she wants me to talk. As we jogged along, she showed me the various buildings and told me what they were. I didn't realize that there was a lake by the base.

She jogged effortlessly so I had to asked, "How could you jog and talk at the same time?"

"I did cross country training in high school," she responded.

Quickly I responded with, "I am a sprinter, not a long distance runner."

That was the longest distance I have jogged in a while. I kept hoping that she would stop. Finally, she stopped and I breathe a sigh of relief. Actually, I wanted to stop for a while so I could catch my breath. We started to walk the rest of the way and then she turned to look at me.

"Are you all right?" she asked.

"Yes I'm fine," I replied.

"Then why are you breathing so heavily?" She pointed out.

I was slightly embarrassed, so I was silent for the rest of the way. As soon as we get to the building, we exchanged our names and asked each other about our backgrounds. She thanked me and we said our good-byes. I couldn't wait to rest my tired aching body and catch my breath.

I did not know who she was. I have never seen her before. It was as if, she appeared out of nowhere. Then, I found out she was two classes ahead of me. As the classes moved up, we were transferred to a dormitory closer to the school.

It was time for my class to move over to the dormitory. My classmates and I had to pack our things and move our luggage over ourselves, which was a long haul. I was so tired when I arrived, only to find out that our rooms were on the top floor and there were no elevators. I dreaded climbing those stairs because my bags were heavy. Then, out of the corner of my eyes I saw the young lady who I volunteered to jog with, flashing a big smile.

"Hi, Sophia, do you need any help?" she asked.

"If you want to, but the bags are...."

Before I could get the words out of my mouth, she lifted my sea bag with ease, took it up several flights of stairs and came back down to help me with the bag I was carrying. I was shocked, usually when people are very attractive, they act as if they cannot lift any thing, yet she took the heaviest bag. I never met a person like this, who was genuinely unselfish and kind, besides my great grandma.

Then, I found out she was wild and out going and I was tame and quiet, yet we both had the same inner qualities. We were both apologetic, considerate and had a childish sense of humor. We became friends after that.

It was early one morning and I was in bed. One of my roommates was on watch that night. She told me that my friend got into trouble last night. I did not have to ask who it was; I just got out of bed, put on some clothes and went to her room. She was crying in her uniform, with her eyes puffed up.

"Why are you crying and why are you in your uniform?" I asked.

"Because I now have to muster with the flag bearers every day, when they raise the flag," she cried.

"What happened last night that is a harsh punishment?" I wondered.

"I was drunk, so I took a cab back. When we got here, I threw up in the van, and then the cab driver started to yell at me, and told me that I had to pay. I refused to pay, so they called the highest person in rank that was on watch." She sniffled, wiped her eyes, and cried some more then continued.

"I was feeling very sick, and they made me get a bucket of water and a sponge with some disinfectant and clean it up. I got angry and said some bad words, because I didn't feel good. Now, I have to muster three times a day, and meet in the classroom for two hours after class," she continued to cry.

"They even take my civilian clothes privileges away, now I cannot go anywhere," she squealed.

"You're always getting into trouble, but this time I think you've out done yourself," I replied.

Previously, her civilian clothes privilege was taken away for wearing her hair down in uniform and she was also confined to the barracks, now this was even worse. The only thing I could do for her was, to tell her to read the 27th Psalms, which she appreciated.

Since she was confined to the dormitory and I never usually go anywhere we were forced to get to know each other better. We would talk for hours about every subject and I found her honesty shocking. She was very straightforward and emotional and I was very reserved and kept everything inside.

I discovered that she was going through a lot, which caused her to break down emotionally. That explained the erratic behavior pattern she displayed. On occasion I would tell her that I found it odd that we became friends and that normally I would not talk to someone with her personality, but she was different. I was the type that gets embarrassed easily.

Gradually, I let my guards down, but I was still very reserved. She was invited all over because of her popularity, but she would insist that I go with her. Even though I had my civilian clothes privileges, to make her not feel bad, I would wear my uniform also.

Finally, her punishment was over, with civilian clothes privileges attached. It was as if she never had freedom before.

We went everywhere. I would say no, she would say yes, and soon you never see one without the other.

One day, she became ill and had to go to the hospital. I tried to cheer her up by visiting almost everyday. When she came out she announced to everyone that I was her best friend and I did the same.

Corps school was almost over and she thanked me for my support and being a true friend. I returned the complement to her by letting her know how much she has influenced me.

I confessed, "Normally I would not talk to or associate myself with anyone, who I think did anything that I considered bad. But I have learned how to be a better friend, because I have made some mistakes in the past, and lost my best friend in high school, because I judged too much."

I told her about my best friend in high school, whom I met in junior high. When I first came to this country, she was the first to be-friend me and taught me the American way of doing things. One day I asked her what she wanted to be when she grows up. She told me she wanted to be a mother. In my mind I thought that she did not have any ambition. I did not say anything to her, but it was in my thoughts. It was very wrong of me.

We graduated from junior high and transferred to high school. One day I saw a pregnant teenager in school and I was shocked. I told my friend that she had the nerve showing up in school, with a big belly like that for all to see. It was very wrong of me.

A year later, my friend was acting funny and I did not console her. I did not ask anything personal, unless the information was volunteered to me. I kept personal things to myself and expected others to do the same.

One day, my best friend's mom called me and told me to pick her daughter up for school. I did not even give it a second thought, even though we usually meet at the bus stop. I went up to the house and her mom let me in. I attempted to go to my friend's room but the door was locked. That was unusual; I have never been to the house and saw her door closed before. I went and sat around the table and waited patiently.

Her mom passed by, so I asked her if her daughter was alright. She told me that her daughter was feeling sick. Finally, my friend came out of her room, with a forced smile.

Her mom told me, "Make sure that you take her to school with you and make sure she gets back home with you, personally."

We both went to school and there was silence between us, so we did not say anything to each other. It was fifth period and we both had the same class. My usual seat was in front of her. Before the class started, I felt a feeble tap on my shoulder. I looked towards the direction of the hand and it was another classmate.

She said, "Your best friend has something to say to you."

Before I could turn my attention to my friend, I noticed that everyone got silent and was staring at us.

Cautiously I said, "What's wrong?"

"I have something to tell you, but promise me you won't get upset," my friend urged.

The whole class leaned forward to hear, what was being said, so I panicked.

"No! What's the matter? Tell me! Is there something wrong?" I pleaded.

"Make a wild guess!" she replied.

I thought about it and said, "You don't want to be friends with me anymore."

"Oh Sophia, of course not, I'm pregnant!" She exclaimed.

"Will you stop fooling around," I warned as I turned myself back into position.

Several people nod their heads and exclaimed, "She is!"

I turned back around and said, "I don't believe you!"

She lifted up her shirt enough to expose the elastic waist pants she was wearing. I looked in shock!

"Now, do you believe me?" she replied.

"Yes! I believe you, I really do believe you," as I turned back around.

I was very hurt, she was five months pregnant and I did not have a clue. That goes to show you how much I did not involve myself in the personal lives of my friends. Everything was fun and games for me. I did not think I was a good friend, because she did not confided in me.

After school, I waited for her and I made sure she took the bus with me, and personally escorted her home. I did exactly what her mom told me to do. The bus ride and escort was voided of conversation with the exception that I asked her if she felt o.k. There I was, always the consummate professional.

Then, I remembered the remarks I made about the other pregnant teenager I saw in school, no wonder I was the last to know. Our friendship ended eventually as we grew apart. I did not know how to handle emotional situations.

It was time for my new best friend to graduate from Corps School. I was not far behind from graduation myself, but we kept in touch. After two years of one visit, exchanges of letters, postcards and numerous hours on the telephone, she was like a sister to me. It was almost six months to a year that I did not hear from her, but I continued to write anyway.

Finally, I received a call from her. She told me that she was getting married and wanted me to be her maid of honor. After I found out what a maid of honor was, I felt insecure.

"Don't you have another friend that could take my place?" I asked.

"No!" she replied.

"What about your sister, a cousin, a family member?" I urged.

"My sister is too young," she answered.

"That is a great honor! Are you sure? You are going to have a lot of people mad at me," I pointed out.

I went on and on trying to make excuses.

"Sophia! Stop it, I want you to be my maid of honor!" she said firmly.

I accepted her request and was honored, but deep down inside I felt insecure. My insecurity stems back from my shyness and I always considered myself a plain ordinary girl from Jamaica. Previously, I was taunted about the shade of my color, the way I looked and I was told I was going to amount out to nothing. I did not understand why she would want to choose me. I did not think or feel that I was attractive or worthy enough to be her friend. After all, she was White and I was Black.

I took a month vacation and went home to visit my mom. During my month's vacation, I visited my best friend for a week. She introduced me to her fiancé and friends, they made me feel welcome. It was at this time she noticed my shy and awkward behavior and knew the cause of it. She pulled me aside and showed me a photo album of friends and family. Then, she came up to this picture, where she was posing with someone who was plus sized.

She then said, "Oh, this is one of my best friends. I loved her so much but she failed to see the beauty she had, inside and out. I could not get her to see the beauty she had. All she looked at was her outward appearance. But I did not care about that, I loved her unconditionally."

I did not respond back, but I knew that was a message for me. Even though at times, I appeared to be confident. Deep down inside I was very conscious of my broad shoulders, big hands and big feet for a woman. In Boot camp, I was told that I stuck out like a sore thumb. I knew that I looked and acted differently than others. Therefore, I tried to blend in with the others.

The more I tried to blend in and be like everyone else. The more I was isolated and scrutinized, as a constant reminder. At one point in my life I hated being me. Now, my new best friend is pointing out my obvious insecurity that I have about myself. I thought about it and she was right. I was very touched; this gave me a boost of confidence. It caused me to view myself differently.

As a child growing up, I took life seriously and had a stiff appearance. My idea of greeting friends was with a firm handshake. This was how close they got to me. I held everyone at a distance. My best friend thought me how to relax, enjoy life and join the human race.

Then, I was given a grand tour of her home state, which put me at ease. I went home feeling special, as I told my mom about my trip.

Several months later my best friend got married. It was the first wedding I ever attended. It was like a fairytale that I read in books as a child. I could not believe that I actually participated in this grand banquet. I had a great time.

The Bible said, "A man that hath friends must shew himself friendly, but there is a friend that sticketh closer than a brother." (Proverbs 18:24) KJV

All of a sudden, my life changed for the better and I thought it was happening by itself. My, how soon I forgot.

CHAPTER EIGHT

MY PERSONAL ENCOUNTER

I was so blinded by ignorance that I could not see straight. I knew there was a supernatural force out there, which is God but I refused to acknowledge Him. I cried whenever I saw innocent kids all over the world starving, war torn countries reduced to rubbles with total disregards for human life, and people being dehumanized because of the color of their skin.

"Why should I take time out of my life, to praise, worship, and idolize a God who let bad things happen to innocent people?" I vowed.

I decided to live my life accordingly, making sure that I do not hurt anyone, being kind, decent, considerate, and a law abiding citizen. In other words if I can sleep at nights with a clear conscience, that was good enough for me.

I was becoming deeply aware that someone is watching over me, I could not see them, but I felt their presence. My love for solitude was comforting. I lived in a one-bedroom townhouse with my best friend a javelin's throw away. My best friend and her husband took the time out to show me how to drive, and I appreciated it very much. I was living in her home state and not mine at the time and we both shared the same views on God.

Even though I had these views on God, I did not pray, yet whenever anything went wrong in my life He was the first one I call. On the cable television I started to watch a couple of Television Evangelist. They were both different and had a radical style of teaching and healing. Then, there was this lady who was a Seventh Day Adventist, who would beat at my door and I would let her in on occasion. She was the one who brought it to my attention about the rulers and principalities of this Earth. This caused me to stop blaming God for everything bad that happens.

I was working in the Open-Heart Surgery department as a Surgical Technician. This required being on call and working long hours. It was very important to have a good vehicle to drive. I had a little old car, that was ten years old, but I loved it. This was my first car and I could not tell you the last time I had an oil change.

Since, I was still on orientation; another person was placed on call with me. I went home from work late and I was very tired. I noticed that oil was leaking from my car and I was low on gas, but I did not have enough strength to take it to a gas station, so I put it off for the next day. Work started at six in the morning, and sleep was my number one concern.

At approximately four o'clock in the morning I was called to come into work for an emergency heart case. I jumped up, brush my teeth, washed my face, got dressed and was on my way. I hit the highway and was going as fast as I could. Then all of a sudden, my car started to slow down, even though I stepped on the gas pedal all the way.

I panicked saying, "Please Lord don't let me brake down on this highway," as I urged my car to go on.

I finally got off the highway and thank God, all the lights were green. Most of the gas stations were closed at that time in the morning. The hospital was almost in sight, but my car was getting slower and slower, until I saw an opened gas station. I pulled over to get some gas.

As soon as I filled up, I was on my way, only to find out that the car needed more than gas. I put some oil in it, started the car and smoke began to escape from under the hood, then it stop moving. It was a good thing that I broke down right by the gas station, where I could make a phone call. I called into work and told them about my predicament, so they sent someone out to get me.

It was a good thing I had someone else on call with me. After work, I had to get a ride home from one of my co-workers. When I got home, I had to face the fact that I needed a new car and I need it now. My savings was depreciated, due to the fact that I had just moved to the area and was unemployed for two months.

My best friend had to take me into work on a couple of occasions, which was too early for her to get up, so I decided to rent a car. I did not have a credit card, so my best friend's husband used his so I could get a rented car. This means that I had to pay cash for the rented car. I rented a car for almost four weeks.

The car dealers could not give me a car, because I had no credit, no down payment and no trade in. I was backed in a corner again, with a problem that seemed hopeless. This time I did not panic, there was a voluntary calmness that covered me, as if to say everything was going to be all right, so I adopted it and turned it into confidence.

One day, I was at lunch and one of my co-workers told me that the Credit Union is giving out loans for new cars, at a low rate and no down payment. He told me to go down and open an account with them and that they had a car show on the weekend, at a specified dealer. I went to the bank, opened an account and picked up a brochure about the car sale.

The weekend arrived so I went to the car dealership, picked out a car and went to the dealer, only to find out that I had to have a pre-approved loan. I thought that all I had to do was pick out a car and they would give it to me, without a down payment because I was a member of the credit union. To make matters worst, it was the last week of sales on new cars.

The following Monday, I went into the credit union to inquire about a loan. They told me that they could not give me a loan because I had no credit history and that I needed a co-signer. I called my mother and she faxed them the necessary information. After a week of uncertainty, I finally got a car loan with no down payment and low interest rate. I have never felt better. I had a new car, a nice townhouse apartment, and an excellent job.

Before I knew it, things started to change. I consider myself to be healthy, when all of a sudden I had a medical problem. I knew this was abnormal, so I shared it with my best friend. She was more worried than I was for myself. I told her that I was not going to go to the doctor. Even though I was in the medical field, I hated to go to the doctor. My best friend would threaten me to go to the doctor and I refused to go.

Even though I did not acknowledge God, I believed in healing. I was now forced to pray, but the problem did not go away. To make matters worse, the case load slowed down at work, so they asked for a volunteer to take the following week off. I quickly took the opportunity, so I could go home and visit my mom. I took a flight home and couldn't wait to get there. Isn't this a coincidence?

As soon as I arrived I started to complain to my mom about my medical problem and asked if she could pray for me. She told me to wait until we get home. Later that night I reminded my mom, so she placed her hand on my tummy and prayed for me, with me believing that the problem would go away. I woke up the next morning and the symptoms were gone. I prayed and thanked God.

My mom was going through a difficult time and again she told me how God has been good to her. She was laid off her job, so she decided to go to nursing school, worked part time and managed to pay the mortgage and kept the house. She was still single and continued to give ten percent to the church. The whole week I was home, my medical problem disappeared. I left having no doubt that there was a God.

When I got back, I was so excited about not having any symptoms that I told my best friend what had happened. As soon as I went back to work, the symptoms started again, but I still refused to go to the doctor. I just pretended as if nothing was happening.

The weeks passed by and we were forced to go home because there was nothing to do. This was a big problem. It was beginning to affect me financially. I could not afford to take a cut in pay, so I took calls almost every weekend. At one point my checking account was so low, that I could not pay for a bill. Then I received a check in the mail from my auto insurance. This was odd because I did not get into an accident or know why I received it. I just praise the Lord and jump up and down.

Then tragedy struck, this is when I found out that my great grandma died. Within several days, I had to go to Jamaica to attend the funeral. I was sad but happy that she went to her place of rest. I came back, spiritually uplifted and wanted to live according to the way she raised me.

Several months later, I went into work and heard that they were going to do a commercial. It was to my under-standing that it was going to be done in a specified room, so I assumed my co-workers in that room was going to do it. My room was one of the first rooms to complete its case. As I walked out, I noticed all the camera equipments and personnel in the hallway.

On my way to lunch, I went to the lounge, ate my lunch and was on my way back. I did not have an assignment, so I stop by the front desk to see if there was anything I could do. They were talking about the commercial, so I listened in. Apparently, my co-workers who were assigned to the room for the commercial went home. Their scheduled time was up, so they were wondering who was going to do it.

I get bored easily, so I went to find something to do. Then, I heard my name called over the intercom to report to the front desk. I went to the front desk and saw my supervisor.

She said, "You're doing it Sophia!"

"Me!" I said with surprise.

"Yes!" she answered.

"Don't you want someone that is a little more attractive?" I asked.

"Oh Sophia! You look fine," she remarked.

Most of my co-workers were very beautiful, and I did not think that I fit in that category, so I went to the lounge and grabbed a friend and took her back with me.

"Look how beautiful she looks! Isn't this the face you want for a commercial?" I exclaimed.

My supervisor said, "You are doing it, get back to the room!"

I finally accepted the fact that I was going to be in the commercial, which I could not believe. After preparing myself, I went back to the room and behaved like a professional.

You're probably thinking, "How did a simple Jamaican girl, who almost failed out of high school, ended up in an Open Heart Surgery department, in a major city participating in a commercial."

My best friend and I use to share the same ideal, in our belief in God. My belief changed drastically, from a question mark to a period.

I told her, "I think there is a God. Even if you have to pray to the nature God, pray and give thanks. There is a presence out there, I don't know what it is, just pray and give thanks."

I wanted to know without a shadow of a doubt, that there was a God. It was as if God said to me, "So you don't want to acknowledge me uh? Well I am going to let my presence be known unto you."

He surely did let his presence known to me; proof was coming in from everywhere. The only thing I could say without a shadow of a doubt is, "There is a God."

I began to realize that God wanted me to go back home, because things were getting a little bit difficult for me to stay where I was. It was enough to get my attention, but not enough to hurt me. I still had a medical problem that I was ignoring. Then, the case load had slowed down at my job.

My best friend and her husband were moving out of state. Then I had some family members, who were coming to reside in the U.S. for the first time. I was left to make a decision, and I chose to move back home. I told my best friend that when I move back home, I am going to start going to church and give my life back to God.

I moved back home, and immediately my medical symptoms disappeared. I was amazed but not surprised. My mom invited me to church again and I went once and did not go back. My major concern was to get a job.

My mom introduced me to most of her friends, included a young lady she claimed she adopted as a spiritual daughter. She was very fond of her and said many wonderful things about this young lady. I talked to her myself and was very impressed. She asked me when I was going to go back to church. I told her when I get myself established.

I cannot remember how the conversation got started, but we were on the subject of tithing. I told her I want to give myself up totally to the Lord, but I cannot perceive giving ten percent of my salary. To me that was a lot of money to give up. She told me that she tithes on a regular basis and that the Lord blessed her beyond her means. She lived by herself in an apartment, had two jobs and was going to college. She simply urged me to tithe.

I thought to myself, "If I wanted to give myself to the Lord one hundred percent, it includes tithing."

It was over two months now, and I got my old job back at the research lab at the hospital. I was just about to run out of money, and not to mention the fact that my kin folks were coming in from Jamaica.

God knows what's best, I needed the rest. At my past job I took calls almost every weekend to make up my salary, and I was physically tired. Now, this job offers me more money and a regular schedule. If God wants you to move, and you move when he wants you to, you can be assured that he has something prepared for you.

Soon, my family arrived, and my aunt and cousin went to church, but I didn't. I wanted to go but I was not motivated.

My mom asked me again if I wanted to go to church, by announcing it was, "Dress down day."

She did not have to repeat herself. I ran upstairs, took a shower and was ready before everyone. We all went to church together and it felt great. The message preached was so clear, that I cheered the minister on. Then, they announced it was going to be, "Dress down month."

I made up in my mind that I was going to attend church the whole month at lest. I attended the next week and the next, and I was surprised. I did not know that the Bible contained all this great wisdom. I never read the whole chapters of the Bible, with the exception of specific scriptures and passages in a great while. The only thing I liked to read was the Psalms. I could not believe it; I was actually excited about church and could not get enough.

One Sunday, my mom got into the spirit; she was speaking in Tongues and dancing. I watched in amazement. When we got home, my mom went into another room so I took the opportunity to imitate her.

I asked my aunt and my cousin, "Who act like this?" as I danced and try to repeat the words I heard my mom uttering in church.

They both laughed, and my mom heard me. The next Sunday, I think she probably didn't want to loose it again in front of me. When she felt the spirit was overcoming her she sat down and tried to stifle off the words. Obviously, she was trying to hold back, I felt bad because I was the one imitating her.

She started to shake in her seat and the words came hurling out. My mom had no choice but to get up and acknowledge His presence. It was as if God was making an impression me with His powers.

I was like a kid saying, "Wow, Amazing!"

The final Sunday for dress down day arrived, and I was truly impressed with what God can do. After the sermon, it was time for the invitation to join the church. Six people went up as the pastor stretch forth his hand. I thought that he would stop because that was enough, but he still had his hands out. Now, there was a voice talking to me personally, telling me to come, but I stood my ground. Two more individuals went up but the pastor still had his hand out.

The voice was urging me to go up, "After all it is the last Sunday for, dress down month."

That got my attention. I broke down and went up to re-dedicate my life to God. I was told that the church offered a thirteen week new believers' series. I made up my mind to attend every week, with no turning back. I started to tithe on a regular basis and I was beginning to acknowledge God even more. I attended the classes and was growing at a fast spiritual rate overnight.

I continued to go to classes and I was still growing at an alarming rate. Knowledge, wisdom and understanding were at my fingertips. During the thirteen weeks of the new believers' series, it was bought to my attention that there was a Bible school at the church. I signed up right in time. That is when I took Intro to Evangelism. We were urged to read our Bibles by one of our instructor.

When the semester was over, it was time for a summer break. I made up my mind, to read the Bible every day. My mom told me to pray particularly for knowledge, wisdom and understanding. My Bible is the, King James Version. The text was so easily understood that, I thought to myself, was all this information in the Bible the whole time. I was upset with myself; everything you wanted to know about life was in it.

Ever since I was a child, there was always a Bible, in all the households I have been. The thought never occurred to me to pick it up and read it for myself in its entirety. Again, I was simply amazed.

On the day, it was revealed to me to acknowledge the fact that I was an Atheist. God took me back through my life and pointed out specifics. Then I realized that God was with me all of my life. I began to fear Him, with reverence.

"The fear of the Lord is the beginning of knowledge: but fools despise wisdom and instruction." (Proverbs 1:7) KJV

CHAPTER NINE

THERE IS A GOD

"Ask, and it shall be given you; seek, and ye shall find; knock, and it shall be opened unto you: For every one that asketh receiveth; and he who seeketh findeth; and to him that knocketh it shall be opened." Matthew (7:7, 8) KJV

CURIOUS MIND

Where am I?
Who made me?
Who am I?
Please don't forsake me.

Like a wondering child
With a curious mind,
My imagination ran wild,
But the visions are so hard to find.

I have millions of questions.
Asked but unanswered?
Is heaven our destination?
Can knowledge and truth be measured?

We live, we die
Grow young and old.
Another mother cries,
Someone took her baby's soul.

When I wrote this poem, it was my quest to find knowledge, wisdom and understanding. God took me back in time and told me to read it one more time. I re-read it and my mouth dropped. I sent out a distress signal, desperately seeking the truth and God stood by my side and guided me through life, showing and revealing things to me. I did not realize it, until it was revealed to me to write this book. Excuse me for a second, but God is awesome. I am simply amazed and flabbergasted.

Now, when I read the poem, I am no longer seeking because I have found the answer. Thank God I do not have to ask, "Where am I?" because I know where I am.

I do not have to ask, "Who made me?" Because I know who made me, without a shadow of a doubt.

No longer would I have to ask, "Who am I?" because I know my purpose.

WHERE AM I?

Deep down inside many of us ask ourselves this question. The majority of you would probably say that the question asked, is relatively easy. The answer is we are on Earth. I know we are on Earth, but my question goes a little deeper. We are natural born curious creatures. I would have to be like a rock cheated out of life, not to notice what is going on around me.

For example, why are there so many of you that are like me around? Why am I not alone here? What is that green stuff that shoots out of the ground? What are those flying creature that goes from here to there, in the air and on the ground? Why are those thick, long, pole-like structures with out-stretched arms we call trees, here? What is that structure which springs out of the earth that forms a pattern attracting my attention, and giving off a sweet aroma, we call flowers. I could go on and on.

The fact of the matter is we are on Earth. The question is, how did the Earth came to be? We tend not to accept things as they are. We want a second opinion, while others seek for numerous opinions. If we cannot touch it, taste it, feel it, hear it or see it, it does not exist, and therefore we render it impossible.

As a child growing up, I was told and I became quite aware of the fact that the Bible said, "In the beginning God created the heaven and the earth. (Genesis 1:1) KJV

I could not properly digest what I swallowed. A seed of doubt is planted in my mind, bearing fruits, which have a question sign on them. When you ask questions, it means that there is uncertainty. The answer was right under my nose, yet I seek a second opinion. Therefore, the question still floated around.

We all wonder, "How could God create such an awesome splendor?"

I stop searching because I end up right where I started. If the earth created itself, it would be shapeless and unorganized. My brothers and sisters, the fact of the matter is, God created the Heavens and the Earth.

WHO MADE ME?

Some of you would say God, while some of you would say my biological parents. The process which our biological parents are responsible for is, mating. This is the unity between a sperm and an egg, and then we basically sit back and watch it grow. If we came to exist by some biochemical accident or evolution, I am amazed that an accident could organize a whole universe and have everything performing like a cycle. That is some accident, some how I cannot accept this unproven theory.

"So God created man in His own image; in the image of God created he; male and female created he them." (Genesis 1:27) KJV

This is difficult to think that God created us, when we actually see females during pregnancy, and later giving birth to a child.

There is an age-old question, "What came first, the chicken or the egg?"

The answer is in the Bible. Obviously the chicken came first, if the egg came first, who would have incubated the egg and when it was hatched who would have nurtured the chick? That is why Adam and Eve were made first at an adult stage and not an infant stage. The sperm and the egg did not exist until man and woman was made, that contain the cells.

"And God said, Let the earth bring forth grass, the herb yeilding seed, and the fruit tree yielding fruit after his kind, whose seed is in itself, upon the earth: and it was so." (Genesis 1:11) KJV

This answers the question of the chicken or the egg. Every plant life and animal life was pre-made with a seed. Man and woman are also included. We like to separate ourselves from the other forms of life, when in actuality we are direct replicas of them.

Your next question might be, "How were we made?"

"And the Lord God formed man of the dust of the ground, and breathed into his nostrils the breath of life; and man became a living soul." (Genesis 2:7) KJV

Why is this so hard to believe? We have so much in common with plant-life, and we do not even know it. A plant springs forth from the dirt of the ground. This is a part of the earth. We are formed from the dirt of the ground.

The dirt of the ground is a substance that supports and sustains life for both plants and humans. Take a look at your bodies and take a look at plants. Plants need the dirt of the ground to anchor its roots, to sustain its life. God formed us from the dirt of the ground, Therefore our roots are anchored on the inside. We call our roots vessels, which are arteries, veins and capillaries.

The roots absorb nutrients from the dirt of the ground and it is distributed to the rest of the plant. Our vessels absorb nutrients into our roots, which we call the blood stream and it is distributed to the rest of the body. My brothers and sisters we are walking, breathing, living, molded dirt of the ground.

Plants have seeds that are external and we have seeds that are internal. In order for a plant seed to survive, its roots have to be anchored with water, sunlight, nutrients and carbon dioxide present. A plant needs help from nature to bear fruits and produce an offspring, because of its inability to move around freely.

We are responsible for the union of our seeds, with the ability to move around freely. Our seeds unite internally, becoming one. Then it anchors itself to the pre-made molded dirt of the ground, in a female's body.

In order for our seeds to survive, its roots have to be anchored with water, nutrients and oxygen. Where else can a seed survive, unless it is anchored in the dirt of the ground? Think! My brothers and sisters do not get caught up with other theories or hypothesis.

Theory is the scrutinizing of God's creation, using a hypothesis because of one's rights to freedom of speech, undermining the Creator, claiming His works as your own, others or spontaneity, which therefore leads to discredit. We all get furious when someone takes credit for our own personal idea or work. How do you think God feels about this?

Scientist and observers need to realize that you cannot make up or give an account for what happen before we were born, by sample analysis. I could write a poem that is so complex that the readers might all interpret it differently. Until I expose what I was really writing about, the readers are using a hypothesis. The most ironic thing is that even if I expose its true meaning, some may challenge my own interpretation.

"For my thoughts are not your thoughts, neither are your ways my ways, saith the Lord. For as the heavens are higher than the earth, so are my ways higher than your ways, and my thoughts than your thoughts. For as the rain cometh down, and the snow from heaven, and returneth not thither, but watereth the earth, and maketh it bring fort and bud, that it may give seed to the sower, and bread to the eater." (Isaiah 55:8-10) KJV

There is nothing wrong with learning about science. The danger is the misconception when it is presented alone and taught as facts. Words that are misleading should be high-lighted and presented as "Theory" and "Hypothesis". These two words have ruined mankind, because we do not know its true meaning. I have heard it time and time again that the Bible is man-made, when it is a collection of data and facts that occurred throughout history. The only thing man-made is the theories and hypothesis, we are forced to duplicate exactly, when we are taught in schools.

Then some have the nerve to say that religion is forced on them. The underlying truth is science and other man-made theory governs and is forced on you. If religion was forced on you, then, why are you confused and is on the verge of moral decline?

"These are the generations of the heavens and the earth when they were created, in the day that the Lord God made the earth and the heavens, And every plant of the field before it was in the earth, and every herb of the field before it grew: for the Lord God had not caused it to rain upon the earth, and there was not a man to till the ground." (Genesis 2:4-5) KJV

This is the biggest evidence, God created plant-life before He made other living things. Plant-life releases oxygen, which supports other forms of living things. God therefore made other living things after the atmosphere was enriched with oxygen to support us. There shouldn't be any form of doubt about, who made you?

WHO AM I?

The question, "Who am I?" is one of the most difficult questions to answer. If most of us knew who we were, we would not act the way we act or treat each other the way we treat each other. If I had read my Bible and went to church more often, I would have learned more, avoiding countless of hours torturing myself.

I was aware of the fact that I was given a name by my parents, and I am called a human being of the female persuasion. I can think, laugh, cry, love, run, walk, sit, talk, dance and sing. What separates us from other living species or why are we different? If you think you are here for no particular reasons think again. I am sure you notice the difference between animals and humans.

We are made in the image of God. This should show you how special we are. This is truly an honor. I am created in the image of God. I was made by God and I am a descendant of Adam and Eve through adoption. Notice that the verse stated that, we are images and likeness of God. It did not say that man was made a god, we are a mere imitation. We became like the gods, as a result of partaking of the tree of knowledge of good and evil. Some use their knowledge for good and some use it for evil.

"For though there be that are called gods, whether in heaven or in earth, (as there be gods many, and lords many,) But to us there is but one God, the Father of whom are all things, and we in him; and one Lord Jesus Christ, by whom are all things, and we by him." (1Corinthians 8:5-6) KJV

What amuses me is that we are amazed at what humans are capable of making. When the Wright brothers made the first airplane, we thought it was pure genius. When Ford made the first automobile, we also thought that it was pure genius.

Now, we are no longer amazed due to the fact that it can be duplicated. There are several different manufacturers of planes and automobiles. I am amazed at the ingenuity, but you know what would impress me, if things that are man-made could reproduce.

When God made all living things, they came with a seed to produce an offspring. I wish that when I purchase a car, it had the capability of reproducing. Can you imagine all I would have to do is mate it with another car? By the time my car gives birth and the baby car grows up, I mate it with another car, which guarantees another one. This is what makes God, God and us a mere imitation.

Sometimes we take credit that is not due to us. I often hear individuals taking the credit for the making of a baby. We still do not get it in our heads that God made all living things. Did you make your own sperm and egg? Did you give the fetus its heart to pump the blood? Did you make the placenta or put the fetus in a protective sac to regulate its temperature?

Some of us refuse to give God the credit. We search from high to low and from here to there. If we do not take credit for producing our offspring, we take credit for ourselves. The answer is no, if you know of anyone who can make a baby, without tampering with God's creation, please let me know.

"Know ye that the Lord, he is God: it is he that hath made us, and not we ourselves; we are his people and the sheep of his pasture." (Psalms 100:3) KJV

People's lack of acknowledgment to God, is due to not wanting to submit ones self. They do not know who they are, so there is no sense of belonging. What confuses people is their inability to see God because God is a Spirit, so they focus on what they can see.

Until I began to focus on things that are unseen, the concept of God became clearer. We are God's creation that He made from His image and likeness. No one owns you and you do not own anyone else. In other words, we are God's private property.

If you cannot submit yourself or if you do not think that you are the property of God, please stop here. That is why we search for second and third opinions, because we do not want to give credit, where credit is due.

"For whether we live, we live unto the Lord; and whether we die, we die unto the Lord: whether we live therefore, or die therefore, we are the Lords. (Romans 14:8) KJV

We all come into this world, in awe of it. The biggest thing that impresses me so far is the ability to reproduce. Hold a seed of a plant in your hand, and look at a plant that is already grown; now that is a miracle. If you keep the seed without planting it, more than likely it will not grow. A seed is so simple, yet it is a network of sophistication and someone has the blue print. That someone is God, who also has the blueprint to eternal life.

If I can watch a miracle grow up in front of my eyes, what can possibly stop me from believing in God? I believe in God because of the Words of the Bible and my own personal encounters. Do not let anyone stop you from believing in God. Everything else is just a theory-based hypothesis.

Another thing that amuses me is the fact that on the Periodical Chart, there are almost all elements listed known on Earth. There are two elements that are present on Earth, but it is not listed on the chart. They are soul and spirit. Why haven't they been on the periodical chart? A scientist cannot capture it or place it in a container, yet it could go through anything. It is odorless, colorless and indestructible. These have eluded Scientist over the years so they fail to recognize them, like they fail to recognize God.

The fact of the matter is, "They are both the property of God."

If you discover a person who is unconscious and you administer artificial respiration. Chances are the person might recover, with another it might not work. You can administer artificial respiration morning, noon and night, the person will not recover. Oxygen plus soul, equals a living soul. Oxygen minus soul equals death. All you are left with is a vessel that is made of dirt of the ground, and dirt of the ground it will return. While the soul and spirit finds its way back to its rightful owner.

CHAPTER TEN

THE SECRET TO LIFE

I find it amusing when we search all over, trying to find the secrets to life. We buy books, tapes, meditate, travel to far countries and do the latest fad. We try to find it everywhere, except for in the Bible. Well search no more! The secret to life is knowing the difference between good and evil.

> "And out of the ground made the Lord God to grow every tree that is pleasant to the sight, and good for food: the tree of life also in the midst of the garden, and the tree of knowledge of good and evil." (Genesis 2:9) KJV

This is a perfect example of why I believe in God. There is a tree of life and a tree with the knowledge of good versus evil. God thinks in terms of seeds, planting and reproducing. Every living thing that God made reproduces itself. That is why God is everlasting and will reign forever.

Adam and Eve were made without sin, which means that they did not know the difference between good versus evil. The reason why I stated that they did not know what was good or evil was that God had to tell them what to do. They were not aware of themselves because they were spiritual beings. It means that if you and I were to look at them we would not see them with our naked eyes.

> God told Adam and Eve, "But the tree of knowledge of good and evil thou shalt not eat of it, for in the day that thou eatest thereof thou shalt surely die." (Genesis 2:17) KJV

God made us but he did not enslave us. Adam and Eve were given a choice. They could eat of the tree of life and live forever or eat of the tree of knowledge of good and evil, and risk dying a spiritual death.

The enemy appeared to Eve in the form of a serpent, and entices her with the benefits of eating from the tree of good and evil. They had a choice, but the lure of self edification caused them to go against the will of God. The serpent deceived Eve and used them, to get back at God. This is how the enemy operates, he was jealous of their security in the Garden of Eden, so he brought them down with himself.

There are people who will do anything to prevent you from succeeding. They will tell you lies which will deceive you and ultimately leads you astray. Not only did the serpent deceive Eve, Adam also became involved. Adam had the choice of standing by the God who made him or disobeying His command. Adam made the choice to go along with Eve.

It is like a scientist that does not believe in God, who constantly tries to lead you astray with theories, based on a hypothesis. Every time your faith in God is solid, they dig up another bone.

You must remind yourself, "What did God say, not what did man say?"

That is why I refer to sin as a disease, because it causes a chain reaction. The enemy is jealous of God, because he wants to be the one with the blueprints. He wants to be the one who is worshipped and adored. This led him to manipulate most of the angels to try to dethrone God. Lucifer was a leader, but he did not want to humble himself and become a follower. We all want to lead but we do not know the way.

I can imagine Lucifer's sales pitch to the angels, "Aren't you tired of obeying the rules and regulations? Who does God, think He is? Why can't we lead our own lives? If we get the blueprints, we can overthrow God and I will become your leader. Am I not the brightest of the morning star? If I was your leader, you can get to do anything your hearts desire. There will be no more rules and regulations."

I do not know about you, but it sounds like the way most of us think. We want to do whatever we want to do without having to answer to anyone. My brothers and sisters we should always consider the circumstances. God knew that without order there will be chaos, and where there is chaos, there is no peace.

The greatest tragedy is that Lucifer and his followers are immortal, they partake of the tree of life to live forever. This is a perfect example of the fact that when God promises anything he does not go back on his word. So God cast them from His presence and told them that, they are free to live the way they want to live, but not in his place.

When Adam and Eve partake of the tree of good versus evil, they became visible to the naked eyes. They probably could have partaken of the tree of life and live forever, but God intervenes immediately. God told them that they would die, when they partake of the tree of knowledge of good and evil. He did not go back on His word.

Now that Adam and Eve died spiritually, they became visible with the naked eyes. Then God sent them out of the garden, so that they can live their lives the way they want to, but not in His protective custody. The tree of life was then isolated from man.

The Bible warns us of our ignorance, "Lest satan should get an advantage of us: for we are not ignorant of his devices." (2nd Corinthians 2:11) KJV

My brothers and sisters do not let the enemy use you to get back at God and make you miss out on the promises of eternal life. Adam and Eve probably never partake of the tree of life, because it did not look savory. This is how the enemy presents himself, he appeals to the senses without mercy.

The fact of the matter is, the enemy has no power or authority over us. It is a spirit that is unseen with the naked eyes, but the enemy enters our thoughts, dreams and imagination. This is the bearer of evil deeds and thoughts that comes in the form of jealousy, pride, lust, greed, laziness, gluttony and anger. This is the opposite of good, which intertwines with our senses to appease our need for self edification. This uses sight, sound, taste, smell, and feeling to appeal to our senses.

Therefore, we fall for satan's devices before we have time to think about the consequences and lose ourselves. How many times have we been enticed by a person, place or thing, becoming entrapped with negative results? Some of us learn our lesson, while some continue down the same path. The devil cannot make you do anything you do not want to do. When things present themselves as easily accessible, be very careful. We are responsible for making our own choice, think before you act.

Fornication is the perfect example of a temptation that will deceive you. If you are a teenager and you just came to grips with your hormones, it is a battle you will never forget. You need to stop and think about the consequence. My answer to premarital mating is, if you love yourself or your partner loves you, it can wait. If you want to mate with someone please give them the honor, courtesy and respect due to them. Marry them, make it legal. Do not use anyone for your own personal gratification.

It has become such a norm, that we accept this type of behavior in our culture. Love is not sex and sex is not love, we all confuse the two. Love is an emotion and sex is merely physical, unless combined. We are defining love as, you give I receive. We are living in an era where love is being bought and sold. If you do not have any money, you can sell yourself for love. If you have money, you can buy love. If you choose not to be bought or sold, you are left without companionship. The way we use and abuse each other is very sick, we all need therapy. This is pathetic but it is true.

The definition of love is when you want to protect your partner, friends, family and associates at all cost, because you do not want them to sin.

I am sure you have heard this one before, "I'm a good person, why do bad things happen to me. I mind my own business and I don't bother anyone. Why does God let this happen?" We all forget about a choice that Adam and Eve made, and God is honoring the choice.

One of our biggest mistakes is thinking that we are perfect, or to self proclaim that we are good. Our intentions are an attempt to isolate ourselves from our other brothers and sisters, thinking that we are without sin, when we all sin on a regular basis.

First, your biggest sin is your selfishness. You fail to recognize that you are not the only one that bad things happen to. You are probably filled with hatred and anger towards your fellow brothers and sisters with no room for forgiveness. You have committed several forms of sin and I have not even begun.

Life is a constant continuous battle, everyday you get up you do not know what lies ahead. It is time we face reality, we are a part of a whole not an isolated piece by ourselves. I just cannot express my love for God. If you know what I know, you would do the same. God is an equal opportunity God whether you are good, bad or indifferent. One of the biggest secrets to life I found in the Bible, which maintains my mind, body and soul is in the fifth chapter of Matthew.

> "But I say unto you, love your enemies, bless them that curse you, do good unto them that hate you, and pray for them which despitefully use you and persecute you; that ye may be the children of your Father which is in heaven: for he maketh the sun to rise on the evil and the good, and sendeth rain on the just and unjust." (Matthew 5:44, 45) KJV

I know some of you might be saying, "What! After all the things, this person said or that person did to me. This is impossible, I can't do that!"

These sums up several devices of satan, making you think evil thoughts and deeds. Our first reaction is anger, and then we become bitter, we even seek to avenge the wrong that was done to us. In other words we take the law into our own hands.

Ask yourself this question, "Who are you hurting?"

We are hurting our chances of having peace of mind. I remember I would get so upset, that I could literally feel my blood forced through the walls of my vessels. I am surprised that I did not blow a coronary artery or a major blood vessel. I had to make a major decision, either I do not allow anyone or anything to get to me, or I will miss out on my chance of eternal life.

Therefore, I choose to overcome evil with good. If someone talks about me and say negative things, I try to recognize the fact that satan uses us to create havoc amongst ourselves. My response is empathy. I would think that the individuals are living such a pathetic life. Why would anyone waste precious moments out of their lives to talk about me or hurt me, without due cause? I must be important to receive such undivided attention out of an individual's valuable time. The most ironic thing is that we all do the same thing to each other, and then some of us have the nerve to get upset. If you are hurt easily by the things people say or do to you, you are as pathetic as they are.

Sometimes we get our feelings hurt, especially by the ones we love the most, which makes it twice as hard to soothe the pain. Analyze the situation before you jump to conclusion. Remember it is one of satan's devices to cause you to loose control and get out of character, which ultimately defeats you and your purpose. Do not respond to a negative with a negative, break a cycle and overcome evil with good.

Someone close to me once said some negative, nasty things about me and to me. The words were like an arrow and I was the target practice. It hurt so bad that I thought it was unforgivable. I did not understand the concept of how someone could be so cruel and demeaning. This is another example of how we let folks get to us and possess our minds. We get angry, bitter, vindictive and enraged, becoming blinded by our emotions that we cannot see.

Whenever we think about the individual, it triggers off an emotion that eats away at the very core of our being. This causes you to hate them. I do not know if you notice, the fact that it drains you physically and emotionally when you hate. I was in such a state that I could not go on with life because I held a grudge that was causing me to dismantle from the core. I was possessed by satan's devices and was hurting no one but myself.

Finally, I came to my senses and forgive the individual. It was like a heavy burden was lifted off of me. I felt peace. Then, I was able to go on with my life, with a lesson learned. If someone hates you, respond with love. If someone curses you, respond with empathy and let them know that you understand their pain.

If someone tries to use you and persecute you, pray for them. Remember that they allowed themselves to become a puppet and satan is manipulating the strings. Ask God to open their eyes and make them become aware of satan's devices. It will only lead you astray.

Forgiving, loving, blessing, praying and being kind to your enemy is one of the most difficult tasks you will ever experience. Jesus came to this world with several intentions, to set an example of how we should live, to demonstrate the power of the almighty, and most of all to sacrifice himself that we may all have eternal life. What makes me love Jesus is His empathy.

When He was on the cross, instead of feeling sorry for himself, he was more concerned about us.

Then said Jesus, "Father, forgive them; for they know not what they do." (Luke 23:34) KJV

He could have cursed us, and changed his mind. Instead he sacrificed himself, because He knew it was only temporary and he was on a mission. Jesus had a guaranteed spot at the right hand of God. He did not let the jeers of mockery, hatred, cruelty, ungratefulness; lies and injustice stop him from accomplishing his task. Beware of satan's devices.

Another secret to life is to never underestimate the power of saying, "NO!"

My final secret to life is following the Ten Commandments and others in the New Testament. The Commandments are so important, that God and Jesus personally delivered them. This is why we should not blame things on God; he did everything in his power to help us without going against His Word. Adam and Eve made a choice.

In the early times God destroyed the Earth by water. He saved Noah and his family with a pair of each animal, to preserve good over evil. He sent prophets after prophets and they ended up dead, because we kill them. He sent his son Jesus and we killed him too. He also provided us with words of instructions.

The majority of us do not read our Bibles. We put it on a shelf for display purposes. There is a church practically on every corner. Have you gone lately? What saddens me is the fact that I am quite aware that I could write this book and show you a path to finding God. It is quite legitimate, but most of you will continue doing the same things.

I could go around, talk, show you signs, and still it will not penetrate the hardened heart of many who are blinded. If the lack of respect for human life continues, the only choice left is to destroy this Earth entirely and go after the real source of evil. Then all the saved souls will live forever.

> The Bible stated, "But if our gospel be hid, it is hid to them that are lost: In whom the god of this world hath blinded the minds of them which believe not, lest the light of the glorious gospel of Christ, who is the image of God, should shine unto them." (2nd Corinthians 4:3, 4) KJV

Please note that a small g is used for the god of this world, which is satan who blinds the minds of most of us. Fight back and claim your rights to eternal life. Open your eyes, ears, heart, body, mind and soul choose good over evil. Save yourselves and pray for those who are lost, because we are all in this together.

.

CHAPTER ELEVEN

OF WHOM SHALL
I BE AFRAID

Fear is an obstacle that restricts your abilities, rendering you incapable which ultimately defeat you and your purpose. Let me describe what fear was like for me. Fear was as if I was held captive with my hands, mouth and feet bounded, then I was placed in a sealed package and had the words, REJECT, CANT, and NO, stamped all over it.

Fear is a spirit of defeat and if not controlled it leaves you paralyzed. Let me stress that not all fears are good, bad or indifferent. You have to know how to identify the difference.

Joining the Navy helped me to overcome some of my deepest fears. I was afraid of failing, getting hurt, losing, taking chances and not being successful. I would analyze everything, if it appears to be difficult or not easily accessible, I automatically did not do it or even try. Once fear sets in, I automatically gave up and told myself that I cannot do it.

As a child in Jamaica I went to the beach, but stayed in the shallow parts. The majority of the girls stayed in the shallow part, while the guys fearlessly wondered out into the deep waters. We would all talk about our fear of drowning, so we wisely didn't cross the line of water that went over our heads.

In high school, it was mandatory to take swimming classes, so I had to or else I would have skipped it. Again, I stayed in the shallow part of the pool, and learned how to swim free-style. When it was time to go into the deep end of the pool, I turned down the offer and stayed in the shallow end. I found comfort and security in the shallow end, because I was in control of the water and me.

When I joined the Navy, I was asked if I could swim. Then I remembered being taught how to swim in high school, but I cheated myself by avoiding the deep end of the pool. Now, I had to tell them that I knew enough to save my life, but not in the deep end of the pool.

Obviously, if you are going to be in the Navy, you are going to have to know how to swim. We were tested for basic swimming skills and had to swim across an Olympic size swimming pool. Then, I found out that we had to jump off in the deep end and swim across the pool on our backs.

We all thought about swimming on our backs, and it sent fear and panic in the hearts of many, as we scrambled for help. It was bad enough that I had to jump off in the deep end. Now, I have to swim on my back. One of my friends tried to show me how to float on my back, but I gave up after sinking consecutively. She told me I need to relax, but how could I relax when I was sinking and had no control over my body. I could not do it, so I gave up and went over the deep end and waited my turn.

Soon, I was next in line and I was instructed on what to do and what not to do. I closed my eyes, jumped off the platform, came back to the surface, tried to float on my back and I sank. I had to be rescued and taken to the side, to get out. I failed and had to be re-mediated for swimming classes.

I went back to our living quarters feeling defeated, thinking it was virtually impossible for me to swim on my back. I thought I was going to fail and get kicked out of the Navy. Soon, my confidence in every test I did shattered, I was consumed with fear.

We had a clothing inspection and I was standing at attention. It was as if I had an anxiety attach, sweat oozed out of every pore of my body, even my palms. Beads of sweat appeared on my face and formed a colony. I think my company commander said it best when he saw me.

He asked, "Do you want a bar of soap to go with that shower?"

I was called into the office and they asked, "What are you afraid of?"

They tried to give me a boost of confidence, but it did not work. Now that I had swimming classes, I started to miss out on important classes and demonstrations, which was essential to me and the rest of the company.

Then, I was fired from being the first section leader. That did not help me at all, it was as if fear was playing target practice with me and was hitting bull's-eye at a consistent basis. Soon, my fears were turning into failures.

The swimming classes were very interesting. On our first day we were separated into the swimmers and the non-swimmers. I swam at ease, and my instructor looked at me with surprise.

"You can swim!" he said.

"Yes, but I never went into the deep section or had to swim on my back before," I answered.

Then he replied, "Oh, it's easy!"

"Easy!" I responded.

He said, "Yes, I'll show you!"

He just lay back, with his hands out to his side and floated at ease. It looked easy, so I tried it and sank to the bottom, again and again.

"It is all a matter of technique; you have to arch your backs." He responded.

I arched my back, but I sank again. His final advice, break me free from this task that I thought was impossible.

He said, "Oh! I know what you guys are doing. You are using your bottoms as an anchor and if you do not arch your backs and hold your bottoms up, you are going to sink."

I took his advice and fought very hard to keep my back arched and my bottom up. I stop fighting myself, relaxed and I was actually floating with ease. It was a calm and peace I will never forget. The feeling of weightlessness was very soothing. I remember looking up at the sky and admiring the beauty. It was as if I was set free. Just when I was getting comfortable, I was told to go to a deeper section of the pool.

I went to the different levels of the pool until I was at the end, and was able to swim and keep myself afloat. Then it was time for the big test, to swim across the length of the pool on my back. I jumped in, came up to the surface, floated on my back and began to swim. I could not see where I was going, but continued to swim until my arms became tired. Feeling that the pain was greater than my will to continue, I stopped.

"WHAT DID YOU STOP FOR?" shouted one of my instructors.

"My arms were beginning to hurt," I answered.

"You could have completed the whole length of the pool, but you stop and gave up," he responded.

"But I can't!" I exclaimed.

He said, "Turn around and look."

I stood up, and the water was relatively shallow. Then, I turned around, looked and was mad at myself. If I had continued, the test would have been completed, because I only had approximately six feet to go. I hit the water in anger and got out.

The next day I was determined to go the whole length of the pool without stopping. I jumped off the platform, surfaced on my back and pedaled my way across the pool. My arms were beginning to hurt and I could feel my leg dropping, almost hitting the bottom of the pool. That scared me, because it was cause for failure, so I fought back and made it to the end of the pool without stopping. It was a happy occasion.

After getting over my fear of the water, there were other fears I had to face. It was one test after the other. We had our first academic test, from all the classes I had missed because of swimming and I failed it. Several of us failed the test, so we were given a second opportunity, with the understanding that if we fail, we will be set back to another company.

Fear set in again, all past failures came back to haunt me. My heart acted as if it was caged in my chest and was beating itself against my ribs, trying to get out. The night before the re-test, we were given extra time to study. The next day we got in line to go to the test center.

"If you fail the test, when you get back don't get comfortable, just pack your bags because you are going to be transferred to another company," warned my commander.

That comment did not help matters. I think if I had opened my mouth, my heart would have jumped through it and take off running from the pressure. We went to the test center, took the test and waited for the results. It seemed like it was taking forever, until someone showed up with the results.

We were told that all passed, except for two. Immediately, I thought it was me and dreaded going back to the company. A sigh of relief came over me. I passed, but it saddened me to know that two of our associates had to leave. This affected me personally, because it caused my company not to get an academic flag, we had one too many failures. We were always graded as a group.

Soon, I was fired from being in another leadership role. I volunteered for drill class and after a week I was not chosen. We had the second academic test and I failed it again. I did not go to the classes because I volunteered for drill class and had to go the dentist office. We went through the same procedure again. I went back to the test center to take the test again and passed.

The failure cloud was raining on my head again. I failed two more test, in a performance as a group. We had two tests left, a uniform inspection and another academic test. I made sure that I studied, by staying up late with a study group, but I failed again. Thank God, we received our first academic flag.

Later that day we marched to dinner and had to wait, so my commander took the opportunity to test us for the final performance as a group. He went up and down the lines with flash cards, urging us to tell him what it was. He finally got around to me and I was nervous, but I knew those flash cards without a doubt. He showed me a card and I answered it correctly. I was shown another one, and I answered it correctly again. He probably thought it was a lucky guess.

He said, "You know Jones! You have failed the entire academic test, but some how, you manage to pass the second one. Tomorrow you are going to take the re-test. You know, you just might fail this one!"

He held up another flash card, but I did not like that comment, so I answered it with an arrogant tone. We both knew I had it correct, he briskly walk away without challenging me again. I felt a personal victory.

The next day I went to take the re-test and I did not care if I pass or fail. I even placed my head on the desk and got a nap while I waited for the results. I passed the final test.

"The Lord is my light and my salvation; whom shall I fear? the Lord is the strength of my life; of whom shall I be afraid." (Psalms 27:1) KJV

I had the 27th psalms written on a piece of paper that I would occasionally read. It helps me to get over my fear of my fellowman, but it could not help me at that moment. I realized that I was my worst enemy. I had the spirit of fear, which seized control of my life and wanted to defeat me.

It was almost time for us to graduate from Boot Camp and we had some down time. My company commander was taking and answering any questions that we had. A group of us were sitting on the floor in front of him. I was sitting there at ease, when someone boldly asked.

"How comes Sophia failed so many test and did not get kicked out of the company and others who didn't have as many failures did?"

I sat there shocked and was taken by surprise, while the others nodded their heads in agreement. Then, they mentioned another section leader who was set back to another company and compared her to me. I was also shocked when she was set back because she did not fail anything that I know of.

My company commander quickly responded and said, "The reason why Sophia is here and she is not is because Sophia is a leader and she is also a follower. The other one knows how to lead, but she did not know how to follow."

We all sat there in silence. Little did we know, he was helping me to overcome my fears. Most people fear because of loss of control. We fear loosing control of things, others, and ourselves because our priority is not in order. Once we get our priority in order, then we can control our fears.

The word "control," is a form of false sense of security, something that you never had in the first place. Before you were conceived, you did not have a choice whether you wanted to be born or not, if you wanted to be a boy or a girl, who your parents were or what they would look like. You did not know their color, height, weight, ethnic background, social status or physical attributes.

I know that some of us would have liked to be given the opportunity to choose. Wouldn't you like to choose what you would look like and to have control over how we live our lives? Let's face the facts; we do not have control of our lives. We think we do, all because of our false sense of security. Our number one priority is to the one who made us, which is God. Once we get our priority in order, we are on the road to recovery from fear. Now, you can say without a shadow of a doubt.

"The Lord is my light and my salvation," because God is in control.

I have read on many occasions that heart disease is the number one killer in the U.S., I totally disagree. The number one killer in the U.S. if not the world, is fear. If you combine all the statistics, when you uncover the hidden truth for the cause of death, most people died because of fear.

Most of the times in the case of drowning, people drown when panic and fear set in. Smoking cigarettes usually develop into various forms of diseases. This includes heart disease, lung disease and cancer, which leads to death.

Usually, when you ask people why they smoke, the answer is always the same. Whenever they feel nervous or stressed, it calms them down. Fear usually turns into stress and nervousness is a form of fear. Most people, who commit suicide, did it, because fear made them feel like they cannot cope with what life offers.

Fear caused millions of Jews and many others in the world to die, because no one stood up to Hitler, when they had a chance. Fear instills a false sense of security in the heart of a racist and also their victims.

"For God hath not given us the spirit of fear; but of power, and of love, and of a sound mind." (2 Timothy 1:7) KJV

The truth about fear is that it is a demonic spirit, which causes self-destruction. This is another form of satan's devices. Fear strips you of your belief in God, so it leaves you wide open for the enemy to seize control of your emotions through fear. It is the enemies will, to destroy you no matter what.

I guess some of you have been wondering, what have been happening to us? Things are not the same anymore. We have become more lawless with little respect for life. We are allowing the enemy to defeat us through fear, which is why it is the number one killer.

I once mention in the beginning that we are under surveillance, by unseen forces. They have the ability to see us but we can't see them. It is time we recognize, who or what the enemy is. It is not easy to overcome fear; you have to control it before it controls you. Fight back and claim your victory.

"When the wicked, even mine enemies and my foes came upon me to eat up my flesh, they stumbled and fell: Though an host should encamp against me, my heart shall not fear: thou war should rise against me, in this will I be confident." Psalms (27:2, 3) KJV

Take an honest look at your lives. Is God the head of your household or do you hold that position? Do you give someone else the authority to control your life instead of God? Are you making your peers, leaders and associates your god?

Well, I think it's time to fear and panic. Most of us don't realize this; we do not put God first in our lives. When fear sets in, who do we run to first? We run to our families, friends, sex, drugs, alcohol and tobacco. We look for an escape route, instead of running to God. Why do you think the enemy is fighting so hard to make the Ten Commandments obsolete? They are God's solution versus the enemy's solution.

The enemy knows when fear and panic set in, then moves in for the kill. To comfort you, the enemy uses drugs, sex, alcohol and tobacco to ease the pain. Before you know it, the enemy seizes control of you in the form of an addiction. I guarantee you that this solution will always lead you to a path of destruction.

> Jesus said, "Come unto me, all ye that labour and are heavy laden, and I will give you rest: Take my yoke upon you, and learn of me; for I am meek and lowly in the heart: and ye shall find rest unto your souls: For my yoke is easy and my burden is light." Matthew (11: 28, 29, 30) KJV

Jesus is God's solution. I use to be paralyzed with fear, until I recognize it is the work of the enemy. The words that use to frequent my vocabulary were "I can't". Now, I have the power and authority to defeat the enemy, in the name of Jesus. I know without a shadow of a doubt I can do anything that I want to achieve.

I use to fear rejection, until I realize, I am not here to please man, but a God who rejects no one who place their trust in Him. Now, the only rejection I fear is not being able to live in the Kingdom of Heaven and have eternal life.

> The Bible said, "And fear not them which kill the body, but are not able to kill the soul: rather fear him which is able to destroy both soul and body in hell." (Matthew 10:28) KJV

CHAPTER TWELVE

FAITH

Failing typing in high school seemed insignificant, but it became the most significant, because it reflected what I lacked in life. Sometimes things seem easy or self explanatory, when it is a complex piece of a puzzle. If it is applied, it fits perfectly together. I was consumed with fear, which caused me to loose faith, therefore I failed.

Typing was a relatively easy course in high school. I took the course to gain an essential skill that was necessary to learn, not that I wanted to. This is how most of our relationship with God started; we accepted the invitation just to be on the safe side.

Religion requires discipline to be an effective part of our Christian life. This includes, memorization of scriptures, applying the scriptures to our daily life, and having faith.

Typing requires the same discipline. To master the technique you have to memorize the keys, apply proper hand placement, and you have to trust yourself even though you cannot see the keys. The difference is, in religion you have to put all your trust in a God that you cannot see to be effective.

To become an effective typist, you have to start by placing your fingers on the designated keys. You have to know where the letters are, whether it is up, down or on the sides. Keeping your eyes on the assigned work is very important. This is a difficult task and the only way to complete your task in a timely manner.

First, you start off by practicing. Type a single letter, then the alphabet, then a word, which leads to a sentence, then a paragraph. Your fingers take the place of your eyes, giving sight to feelings. This is accomplished by copying word for word from a book, transmitted visually to your brain, then impulses to your fingertips.

To make matters worst you are timed to see how many words you can complete within a minute. Trust is a key factor in mastering the technique for typing, if you do not trust yourself you lack the confidence needed to complete the task.

To become an effective Christian, read your Bible, follow the commandments, and the most important thing is having faith. When you read your Bible it gives you instructions. If you follow the instructions and apply it to your daily life, things fall into place. Knowing that you have followed the instructions, you should be prepared to receive its promises, which comes by faith. You can see the Words, but you cannot see God.

If you study the Bible, the Words are transmitted to your brain visually, sending out impulses all over your body, and if you believe, you can feel the presence of God. Faith is knowing that you cannot see God, but you believe that He exists. A Christian's belief is based on faith, without faith you cannot benefit from the promises of God.

I failed typing because I did not trust myself, for fear of making a mistake. I was given an assignment, to test for speed and accuracy. First I would panic, then, I would look at the book that I was typing from and tried to memorize the words or sentence. The instructor told us to start, and then I turned to look at the keys and type to ensure that I did not make a mistake, which defeats the purpose.

After one minute, I read what I wrote and it was perfect, so I gave it to the instructor. The next day when I got my paper back, I received a failing grade for not completing the minimum words per minute. I cheated myself by looking at the keys while I typed, wasting time looking back and forth. The end result was failure. I was embarrassed when I failed a relatively easy course, which could have been prevented, if I had taken the time to study and memorize the keys in the beginning.

Where there is fear there is no faith. This is my primary reason for writing this book. There are a lot of people who like to take short cuts. When things get difficult, we take the easy way out. This ultimately defeats the purpose. We were all given the Bible, which have the instructions for life. If we had taken the time out to follow the directions, we wouldn't be in the act of moral deterioration, searching for answers already in existence.

The first thing to go is our faith, when we are consumed with fear. This is how demonic forces constantly defeat us. Most of us claim that we trust in God, yet we cannot stand to face the test of time. The reason why we fear the consequences are; we do not realize what a good God we serve.

If you have not come to the realization of God and His capabilities, you are spiritually blinded from lack of intake of the Word. How could we believe in God and do the things we do, when we have the power and authority to defeat all forms of evil that come against us.

We take short cuts and leave ourselves wide open and fall prey to demonic forces. Most of us do not have the time to read our Bibles everyday, but if you are familiar with the scriptures, you can recite the words in your heart, no matter

where you are. When you familiarize yourself with the scriptures, apply it to your daily life.

Most people can quote the scriptures, but have the words
stored in their brain instead of their heart. This is not going
to work. You are only cheating yourself, by taking the easy
way out. No wonder fear has us at its beckoning call, we lack
faith.

Sometimes your thoughts and the things you say can
speak its way into existence. I use to think that I could not do
certain things. Therefore, I did not accomplish what I wanted,
because I spoke against myself. We curse at others and say
negative things towards each other, speaking things into
existence. Parents should be especially careful what they say
to their kids, husbands or wives, your brothers and sisters,
friends, family and associates. If you refer to someone as
being something negative, they might turn into the person
you cursed them to be.

Again, if you allow yourself to fall a victim to someone
else's negativity, you are as pathetic as they are. It is when
you succumb to the negative things they say about you and
think that it is true, which defeats you. Take the negativity as
a challenge and reverse its effect with positivity. This is why
you need to get under the protection of the Lord, do not wish
anything bad against others.

> "But without faith it is impossible to please him:
> for he that cometh to God must believe that he is,
> and that he is a rewarder of them that diligently seek
> him." (Hebrews 11:6) KJV

This is another one of my favorite quotes from the Bible;
it is the epitome of Christianity. You cannot refer to yourself
as a Christian and lack faith, "You might be an Atheist." It
is the difference between light and darkness, there is no in
between. If you join the religious faith, just to be on the safe

side you are making a sad mistake. Either you believe in God or you do not believe in God.

How would you feel, if you created an entire universe and its species and gets no credit for it. Then someone who you think knows you and speaks on your behalf, yields to the doctrine of a scientific hypothesis. You demonstrate your unconditional love, by sending your son to die for a world that has turned its back against you. People only call out your name when they need help, and do not acknowledge you most of the time.

One day out of the week, you are the greatest of all times, and on other days they do not know you. If anything goes wrong in their lives, they blame it on you. You made the Earth and its people and even provided a manual on how to live, and they continue to do the same evil things. Even though we behave the way we do, God still makes Himself available and forgive us, even though we do not deserve it.

Then, I claim to be a Christian who is an avid reader of the Bible, who goes to church on a regular basis, fear and leave myself wide open for the enemy to desecrate the temple of the Lord. The fact of the matter is can you stand by His Word no matter what the circumstances might be?

When others tell you that anything is impossible, you know it is possible with God. When I am down to my last dollar and my bills are pilling up, I remain calm because I know the God I serve, relief is around the corner. When people talk about me, I am flattered because I must be important or doing something right. When the odds are against me that is when I am comfortable, because the sweeter the victory.

I know without a shadow of a doubt that if I stumble or fall, God is there to catch me. When people plot against me, why should I fear when the King of Kings, and Lord of Lords got my back? If everything I own is taken from me, I will not worry over any material possession that could easily be replaced. You can lock me up, through away the keys and isolate me from humanity. As long as I have breath, I will praise the Lord and have faith no matter what the circumstance may be.

If I have a medical symptom, the disease, pain or affliction might as well go away. I will not give into figments of my imagination. If I am hungry, give me a Bible and let me partake of some spiritual food, it is better than bread. There is nothing impossible for God and I know that without a shadow of a doubt. They could dig up new bones and claim that we evolved, I know who made me.

When I wake up in the morning and go to bed at night, I know who is first and last in my life. Since, there is nothing impossible for God, and I put all my trust and faith in Him, there should be nothing impossible for me. Faith allows me to stand on the Word of God and speak it into existence. We have God to back us up and we allow the enemy to use and abuse us at their disposal. If you are a Christian who is consumed with fear and think you are powerless, you are not pleasing God.

When I gave myself to the Lord, I thought that would be the end of my woes. Little did I know that I was going to be attacked. The enemy was trying to find a weak spot by shaking my foundation. I was found to be fearful and panic-stricken. I usually stand and face whatever comes my way, but I try to handle situations myself. Instead I should give it over to God. When you handle the situation yourself, you become emotionally and physically drained, causing you to get out of character. When God realize what your weakness is, He will help to show you the way.

One night, I was stricken with fear wondering what to do. I fell asleep and dreamt that I was in a circular church with a balcony and cathedral ceilings. In the middle of the church there was a lady preaching. Instead of standing behind the pulpit she was floating around in the church. I was looking in amazement, when she asked for a volunteer. Before anyone could volunteer, she floats down beside me and asked me to join her. I thought to myself, it was impossible I will fall. I guessed she sensed my fear and put her arms around my waist and we both floated effortlessly.

I felt at ease and weightless, until she let me go. When I realize that I was on my own, I began to fear. Slowly, I began to float downward, and then a voice told me to remain calm and just believe. I closed my eyes and started to believe that I can float. Then, I floated back up to where the lady was.

We were both excited, and then she said to me, "See! You can do it, you just have to believe."

As I was enjoying the feeling of weightlessness, my alarm went off and I woke up. That was the best dream I ever had, I still have nostalgic feelings about the dream, and it seemed so real. It was not by accident that I had such a dream, in the time when I needed it the most. God is an awesome God.

Please realize that it is up to us to make ourselves available and make time for God. Even though, I totally surrendered myself to God, it is my choice to do what I wanted to do. God do not intervene in your life unless you ask him to, or He will assume that you do not want any help in your life.

Since, I am not ungrateful; I give God his acknowledgment because He is worthy. Some of us get embarrassed easily when it comes to praising God. Now, I do not care who sees me, I hold my hands up, stomp my feet, sing and dance. I have a God to glorify. He did not have to help me, and I could have been a statistic. You have to pray and ask for protection and guidance everyday, because it is a constant battle.

"So then faith cometh by hearing, and hearing by the word of God." (Romans 10:17) KJV

The first time I heard about God, was from others, with the intention of spreading the gospel. I had faith even though I could not grasp the concept of their teachings, it was in pieces. Finally, I picked up the Bible and read it for myself and discover the Words of God. My faith is solely based on His teachings and principles, through His Words. Most people are still baffled, by the concept that God created the Earth and all its contents, when He actually spoke it into existence through faith.

Words are so powerful that we cannot begin to grasp the concept. Where do words come from and what is a word? The Word is God, formulated by Him, to convey a message bringing spiritual things to life, captured on paper, so that it may have everlasting life. Have you ever wondered how the Bible has survived the test of time, when other documents did not?

To communicate is as essential as the air we breathe. Try talking and holding your breath, as soon as your breath stops, so is the words you speak.

"In the beginning was the Word, and the Word was with God, and the Word was God."(John 1:1) KJV

Repeat this quote over and over again, from John 1:1. To have faith you have to grasp this concept. The Word actually existed before the Heaven and Earth were formed. It was a living breathing testament that withstands the test of time. Without the Word, the Heaven, Earth, Moon, stars, Sun, plants, animals, you and me, would not exist. The Word existed, when God breathe life into it, for He was first.

This is what distinguish, God from any of our inventors. An inventor have to come up with an idea, write it down on paper, make a sketch of it, get the materials necessary, make a model and try to bring the finished product to life. It could take days, months and years to formulate an idea.

God created everything by speaking it into existence in six days. Man was made separately. He did not say, "Let there be man." God mold man from the dust of the ground, of his own image and likeness. He did not breathe only life into man, he also breathes the Word into man. The Word keeps us separate from the rest of the animal kingdom, which God gave us dominion over. Have you ever seen an animal, with the vocabulary of a human being that can capture their thoughts, imagination and dreams on any material?

The Word is a Spirit and we should feel privileged to speak it with our breath. That is why we should be careful what we say. The Word is stored in the Bible and is brought forth to life. When we read, it is processed, ingested and stored spiritually, because the Word is God. If you feel like God is far away from you try reading the Word that is manifested by God.

If you watch professional basketball, you will notice that some of the best players talk their way into scoring a basket. On any given night a player could be challenged. If the player backs down from the challenge, they are defeated. Especially if the game seems impossible to win, if the player is determined to win, they can talk it into existence. The player becomes and feels invincible knowing without a shadow of a doubt that every shot that they make, will go in the basket. It is like making the impossible, possible through faith.

I had a similar experience while playing the board game, Risk. The object of the game is to capture the whole world. Each player is given a specified amount of countries, with a specified amount of armies to place on those countries. To be a winner you have to plan strategically and have the dice role in your favor.

I love playing the game because it made me think, so I won on a consistent basis. One day, I noticed that my opponents decided that they were going after me first, so they could have a chance of winning. That was very smart, they took me by surprise.

I was down to one country and the next opponent traded in his cards for a lot of armies and places it right next to the last country I had. I was ready to accept defeat until he started to laugh at me in a mocking tone. I was upset; we made a rule against teasing and talking during the game. I had two armies and he had over twenty-five, the outcome seemed obvious.

"I am going to stampede all over you," he bragged.

"You and what army," I answered.

He laughed, but I was determined not to let him capture my last country, so I spoke the word.

"I will not let you capture this country, I rather let someone else," I scowled.

To beat your opponent, you have to role a higher number than their number. If your country is being attacked, if both you and your opponent role the same number, your country wins. Each time you win, your opponent has to take an army or two off. I had two armies so I was allowed to role two, but the choice was mine. If I rolled two and my opponent rolled two that have a higher number than the dice I rolled, I would instantly be defeated.

My opponent had more than three armies, so he chose to use three dice. The odds were against me, but I did not care, I was determined not to let him win. We battled with the dice for a while and I won each time causing him to take two armies off each time. He could have saved his armies by stopping the attacks, but he wanted me out of the game at all cost.

Finally, he rolled and one of his dice had a higher number so I had to take off one of the armies on my country. Before I could take the army off, he snatched it up and threw it off to the sides. That made me more determined, I was down to one die and one army. He still had a pile of army, and rolled three dice. I must have rolled fifteen or more sixes in a row. His armies were reduced to two.

Instead of quitting he continued and I rolled the last six to defend myself. We were both down to one army on each country. He needed two armies to attack an opponent, but he wanted to continue. We had to show him the rulebook, he could not believe it. I could not believe it myself, everyone stood there in awe.

This was not luck it was an example of speaking the word into existence, through faith. If we have that capability and have demonstrated it time and time again. The possibility is boundless with God. He already gave us the power and authority.

CHAPTER THIRTEEN

SEXUALITY

This is such a controversial subject that I did not want to write about it. I do not know where to begin. Sex has controlled our lives so much, that we have literally loss control of ourselves. We live in a society where everything revolves around sex, and we are pushing it to the limit. How far are we going to go, before we realize, what damage is done to a society that promotes sex?

We are alarmed at the teenage pregnancy rate, yet society is waving a promiscuous flag in their face. They read it in books, magazines, newspaper, leaflets, newsletters, flyers. They see it on the television, billboards, movies, commercials, music videos, the Internet, and in the streets. This does not exclude adults. We are also forced to reckon with the aura, of this thing called, sexuality.

> "For to be carnally minded is death; but to be spiritually minded is life and peace. Because the carnal mind is enmity against God: for it is not subject to the law of God, neither indeed can be. So then they that are in the flesh cannot please God." (Romans 8:6-8) KJV

What is this thing that captivates our mind, body and soul, grabbing our attention and appealing to our senses without mercy? Making us act as if we are hypnotized by its powers, that we become its slave and it is our master. This results in a false sense of security making us think that, we are wanted, loved, attractive, irresistible, charming and powerful. This is one of the biggest hoax that humanity has ever fallen for.

What is amazing is we fail to see the tragic trail we leave behind, when we are under the spell of this thing called sexuality. It would make a man or woman leave their spouse, overlooking the needs and wants of their family, cause a man or a woman to loose every drop of pride and dignity, by prostituting themselves. Even the people of God, who knows the rules, become victims of this thing called sexuality.

We are all to be blamed for allowing ourselves to fall for satan's device. Then, we have the nerve to place each offense in different categories. No one is immune, whether it is incest, child abuse, rape, fornication, homosexuality, prostitution, adultery or pornography. It is all under the same category, and we are all under the same spell. There is no difference; it is all against the principles of God.

Some of us feel abused, taken advantage of, violated and we all want to bring it to everyone's attention. At that particular moment we feel loss of control. Then we turn around and commit the same acts towards another. It is like me accusing someone of taking advantage of me sexually, and then I turn around and go to a night club with male strippers, hooting and hollering for them to take it off, while putting money in their underwear.

When we are in control, we have committed several violations against another person, and probably did not know. It is wrong to go after someone for their looks. It is wrong to go to strip clubs and tuck money in a person's underwear and watch them do things that are obviously without pride or dignity. It is so easy to get caught up in the web of deception.

I am also not immune. Sometimes, we girls behave worst than the guys.

It is wrong to have someone and want another, especially if you are married. It is wrong to engage in pre-marital sex. It is wrong to preposition a person, without the intent of marrying them. It is wrong to prostitute yourself to another. It is wrong to sexually abuse anyone regardless of age.

It is wrong to lie and scheme, just to get someone in bed. It is wrong to use your looks for personal gains by perpetrating a fraud. It is wrong to take advantage of a person, because of their financial or emotional state. It is wrong to parade around in skimpy clothing, when you know its effect. It is wrong to marry someone under false pretenses. It is wrong to substitute love for sex, when there is a difference between the two.

The biggest question is, "Why do we allow ourselves to use and abuse each other?"

It is an addiction when we loose control and do wrong things without considering the circumstance. Most people will tell you, that they cannot go without sex for a certain period of time. This is the biggest lie; it is like saying that we cannot live without drugs, alcohol or cigarettes.

"Are you going to die?"

We have all suffered from some form of addiction. An addiction is when we satisfy our need for instant gratification without considering the consequences, making us feel like we cannot control ourselves. Then we follow along blindly, with our eyes fixated on the object of our desire.

"Flee fornication. Every sin that a man doeth is without the body; but he that committeth fornication sinneth against his own body. What? know ye not that your body is the temple of the Holy Ghost which is in you, which ye have of God, and ye are not your own? For ye are bought with a price: therefore glorify God in your body, and in your spirit, which are God's" (1 Corithians 6:18) KJV

Fornication is sex without a marriage license. Apparently the majority of us do not like ourselves well enough to treasure our bodies. When you first enter puberty, it is very difficult getting accustom, to your new developing body with hormones attached. Your body is the first thing that you called your own.

If you owned a very expensive car, would you let just anyone drive your car, especially if they do not have a license? The answer is, "no". Say the car was given to you as a gift, so you try your best to take care of it. If the person continue to give you reasons, why you should let them drive your expensive car without a license. The answer should still be, no. If the person really care about you, they would not try to put you in that predicament.

In the sixties they spoke of free love. Is it free love or free sex with diseases attached? Free love should be between a disease free husband and wife. When you care or love someone, you handle his or her possession with care. I would not want to drive anyone's expensive car, knowing that I risk damaging their car. With this comes an extensive repair from a psychological view.

Pretend that your body is that expensive car, and you are being pursued. Why would you let anyone use your body when they did not have the courtesy to protect you with a license? They end up running up your mileage, and cause wear and tear on your personal property. You should consider yourself special enough, to want to keep the wear and tear on your body and the mileage down to a minimum.

If someone really love and care about you, their love should over power the sensation that their hormone is giving off. It is a matter of loving someone enough, not to risk causing them to go astray.

Your body is indeed very special, no matter what it looks like. Your body is a specialized vessel, which should be treated like a temple. Do not let anyone cause your temple to become defiled, that the Lord would want to turn away from you. Let them marry you first.

> The Bible said, "Nevertheless, to avoid fornication, let every man have his own wife, and let every woman have her own husband." (1 Corinthians 7:2.) KJV

Fornication sometimes leads to unwanted pregnancies. If you are underage and engage in premarital sex, obviously you are not mature to properly raise and provide a secured home for a child. It takes more than love to raise a child. If the child is not taught from a Biblical perspective, they end up with poor morals and may end up being a statistic.

Most of the time, some may proclaim their love for you and do not live up to their obligation. Quite often women are left alone to bear the burden of raising a child on their own. This is an awful plight. The most upsetting thing is, to hear people say that women get themselves pregnant to trick a man into marrying her. I do not know if people are aware of this, but a woman cannot get pregnant by herself. If the man was not doing, what he should not be doing, he would not be responsible for impregnating a woman.

Prostitution is such a sensitive issue. My empathy goes far beyond the depth of morality. To give up one's body for others to partake of, in exchange for money, favor or drugs is very painful to understand. A prostitute is a lost sheep, whom sacrifice their body to satisfy the lust of the flesh. Is he or she not the brother or sister of us all?

Why do we allow them to fall so low, spiraling out of control? What do they search for, is it love, money, power, sex, or do they really know? Do they love themselves at all, to walk the streets without a care in the world? One becomes a vulnerable target for uncaring and unfeeling individuals, who want to use and abuse your body, because you put yourself out for sale.

I feel empathy for you. We live in a society where we have human vultures, waiting to dispose of anyone's flesh when we are down. This is so pathetic, instead of helping we take advantage and defile a human being. Where is our compassion? Obviously, a person who sells their body needs help. When every bit of pride and dignity is absent, something is definitely wrong with an individual.

If you take advantage of a person in that condition, you are a pathetic form of life. Instead of using your money to help the person, you use it for instant gratification. It is like going to the store and buying a roll of tissue, and then you use it and dispose of it in the trash. This is a crime and it should be stopped. The rich and powerful, apparently likes to buy and sell the property of God. They do not have anything better to do with their money, but to use it to exercise their power.

The bible said, "when the wicked spring as the grass, and when all the workers of iniquity do flourish; it is that they shall be destroyed forever:" (Psalms 92:7) KJV

Adultery is giving yourself to another, when you are married. When you marry someone for the wrong reasons, it usually leads to adultery. If you marry a person for their money, you end up with money all right, but no love. If you marry a person for their looks, you might end up exalting the wrong god.

Do not get married if you think, you are going to be an old maid. Do not get married to avoid fornication; your marriage will be based on sex. Do not get married because everyone is getting married. Do not get married if you know you and your fiancée argue on a consistent basis. Do not get married, if you cannot forgive. Do not marry a person, if they get on your nerves. Do not marry someone who is not sensitive to your needs. Do not marry someone who embarrasses you in public.

This is the most important, if a person does not respect themselves or others, they will not respect you either. It is easy to fall in love, and be a fool. Take the time to choose a partner, and fall in love later. Why marry a person that you cannot talk to and share your dreams, no matter how stupid it is? This is what I do not understand, people who marry in a church and do not practice the principles of God.

The vows say, "In sickness and in health, for richer or for poorer, till death do you part."

It did not say one person benefit while the other sacrifices. Until man and woman realize that marriage is a union of two equal halves. Adultery and divorce will continue to plague our society.

Before I discuss this next issue I would like others to know that I respect the rights of others, to choose what they want to be and what they want to do in life. To be quite frank with you, it is none of our business. God gives us choices and we should allow others to exercise their rights also. But I also have a right to tell the truth, not from my point of view but from a Biblical perspective. No one have the right to disregard any individual because of race, religion, gender, likes, and dislikes, choice or sexual orientation.

God did not tell anyone to take the law into his or her own hands. You cannot act violently towards another because they are not like you. When you are sinning, is there anyone around to see you?

The Bible said, "Thou shall not lie with mankind, as with womankind: it is an abomination." (Leviticus 18:22) KJV

I can respect the rights of people to make their own choices, yet it seems that my rights are some how violated. Do what you want to do with your life. It is when you want us to change the Principles and Commandments of God. This is what I have a problem with, if you want to make up your own man-made theories and doctrines; that is your opinion. Do not try to convince others that the Word of God should change to accommodate the things that it is against.

> "None of you shall approach to any that is near of kin to him, to uncover their nakedness. I am the Lord." (Leviticus 18:6) KJV

Incest is fornication with your next of kin. In the 18th chapter of Leviticus it tells you that the Lord is against incest. You should not uncover the nakedness of your father, mother, father's wife, mother's husband, daughter of your father, daughter of your mother, son's daughter, father's sister, mother's sister, father's brother, mother's brother, father brother's wife or your mother sister's husband.

> The Bible said, "Therefore shall ye keep mine ordinance, that ye commit not any one of these abominable customs, which were committed before you, and that ye defile not yourselves therein: I am the Lord your God." (Leviticus 18:30) KJV

Incest, breech the security of a family's responsibility to provide, a safe environment for their children. So, if you find yourself attracted to your next of kin, you are blinded by lust. Stop immediately, and seek the Word of God and His principles. If you are a victim of incest, remove yourself from the situation and seek help for yourself. If you trust in the Lord, He will take care of you.

"But whoso shall offend one of these little ones which believe in me, it were better for him that a millstone were hanged about his neck, and that he were drowned in the depth of the sea." (Matthew 18:6) KJV

The secret world of children being sexually abused result in a destructive path to maturity. This happens to most adults as children, and the effects are often troublesome. The majority of people, who deviate and accept an abnormal sexual way of life, were abused as children. Their profession includes prostitution, strippers, topless waitresses, X-rated dancers, pornography actors, nude modeling, homosexuality and more.

When one is sexually abused as a child, the victim tends to blame themselves. The feelings of shame and guilt are a living torture. You get feelings of loss of control, being violated, and then you are threatened into secrecy. This result in a psychological turmoil, making you feel that all a man or woman wants from you is sex. Therefore, you automatically give up yourselves thinking that it is a normal and acceptable way of life.

This is confusing to a young adult, who was tainted by a person who was blinded by lust. The young adult enters a path of fornication because they do not know any better. That is why I think it is important to isolate the cause of the problem, so we can better understand why we as a society, breaks down morally.

We try to blame women, for having children out of wedlock. We blame teenagers for their promiscuity. We blame the media and other source of corruption. We are all to be blamed, children learn by example and if we continue to behave the way we behave, it is going to get worst.

If you were sexually abused as a child, my best advice is to forgive and go on with your life, by trying not to commit the same acts against others. If you find yourself going against the principles of God, seek help and gain some self-respect. You are very special in the eyes of the Lord and satan knows this, so he tries to contaminate you through others at a very young age. We must try and stop the cycle, through education. The best way to start is reading your Bible, which contains all the laws, rules and regulations for a decent living.

We are all victims of satan's devices and our own lust of the eyes. The enemy knows our weaknesses, and satan makes it easily accessible. It is up to us, not to succumb to the evil forces of this world that you cannot see. We are going around, doing evil things, thinking that it is normal. I hope we all wake up before it is too late.

We are born with sin and it is inevitable, but there is a way to overcome sin. Choose what is good over evil. Read your Bibles for yourselves, and see what laws you are breaking. Learn to distinguish right from wrong. There should be no excuse for the way we use and abuse each other.

CHAPTER FOURTEEN

AT PEACE WITHIN

I had a dream one night, that I was in a familiar area and there was a car on the side of the street. In the car was a woman sitting stretched out in a vertical position that appears to look like my great grandma. There were some people gathered around her making statements.

They all checked her out and proclaimed, "She's dead!"

I immediately climbed into the car to see for myself. I checked for a pulse and signs of breathing and discovered that she was breathing.

I proclaimed in hysteria, "She is alive, she's still breathing!"

They pulled me away and said, "She is dead, go inside the house!"

I wait by the side, while they placed a box of tissue in the car and wind the windows up. They all walked away from the car and pulled me into the house, leaving her alone in the car. I was very upset, as I paced back and forth in the house. I could not believe that they left her outside all by herself in that condition. My conscience would not allow me to leave her outside like that.

I turned to them and stated, "I don't care what you guys say. I am going outside and I am taking her inside the house. She is not dead, she is alive!"

I went outside, opened the car door, lifted her up in my arms and brought her into the house. I laid her on the bed and she became loose. She was not stiff anymore, and then someone else in the room became stiff in her place. My alarm went off and woke me up. Immediately, I started to pray.

As I get myself ready for work and was heading out the door my mom said, "I just got a call from England. Your grand mother is in the hospital. They said she had a stroke."

Immediately, I remembered the dream and didn't say a word. In the dream, I saw my great grandma who was already dead. To me it was bad news. I acknowledge my mother and hurried off to work. When I arrive at work, I told one of my co-workers the dream I had.

Later that day my mom called and told me we have to go to London immediately, and she was making ticket reservations. In a couple of weeks my mom was scheduled to go on a trip to Israel. I was puzzled; she did not give me a choice, so I had to make arrangements to get some time off. She told me she had to go, because she would not be able to forgive herself if anything should happen to her mother, and she didn't get the chance to see her.

As the day grew closer I felt uneasy about flying. My aunt was also going, so I started having fears of crashing. To make matters worst my Jamaican passport was expired. The picture in it was taken when I was a child. I tried to tell my mom that I cannot make it because of my passport's expiration, but the ticket was already bought. I was definitely in a dilemma with fear and doubt.

I had to talk myself into reassurance and reminded myself the old adage, "Where there is a will, there is a way."

It was too late to do anything about my passport, so I went along blindly. All three of us were at the check-in line at the airport. It was my turn and I was asked for my passport.

I decided to be straightforward, "To be honest with you my passport is expired but I have to go, my grandma is very sick."

"I'm sorry ma'am but I cannot let you go. Even if I let you go, they may stop you in England and send you back!" he exclaimed.

"Well, what am I going to do, it is an emergency and my ticket is already bought?" I asked intently.

"I could cancel your flight for today and re-schedule it for tomorrow at the same time. All you have to do is go to the Jamaican Consulate and request an emergency passport. It is in Manhattan," he gave me some encouragement.

"Can I go now?" I asked.

"No, I don't think so, I think it is closed. You will have to go there tomorrow."

"But I am not from around here."

"If you go down stairs, and go to information you could make a hotel reservation and they will drop you off and pick you up in the morning. Do you want me to re-schedule you for tomorrow?" he asked.

I answered, "Yes."

I looked at my mom and aunt and told them that I would try my best to get there, but I am not promising anything. My mom suggested that I call a family member of mine and stay there for the night instead of paying for a hotel. We called the number and no one was home. I told her not to worry about it I have the money. It was almost time for them to board their flight so they had to go. I quickly asked for several phone numbers and addresses of friends and relatives who lived in England. I wrote them down, and put it in a safe place and waved good bye.

I turned with my entire luggage, took a deep breath and headed downstairs towards information. They set me up at a near by hotel, with a ride to the hotel and back to the airport. I did not plan on spending that much money, but I did not care I was willing to do anything at that point to get to my destination. I made sure I had a good night's rest.

The next day I got a ride back to the airport. It was approximately 12 O'clock noon. Here I am, with all my luggage and I have to go to Manhattan. I quickly came to the conclusion that I was going to put my luggage in storage and pay for it. I didn't want to take it with me, again it cost me.

Now that I was free to move about, I took a cab to the Consulate. Again, I had to pay for the unexpected. I arrived and it was crowded so I picked a number and waited my turn. My number came up so I went up and explain my situation, so they gave me a form to fill out. I filled out the form and waited to be called in. After a long wait my name was called and I went back and explain my situation.

"Well, where's your passport picture?" they asked.

"I don't have any, I didn't know I needed one," I answered.

"Alright, there is a one hour photo mart down stairs and across the street. Tell them you want passport size pictures. You will need four pictures. When you get back tell them to send you right in," she instructed.

It was getting later and later and I was not sure if they were going to give me an emergency passport. I also wanted to call England to let them know, if I was coming or not.

My mind was racing with anticipating thoughts, as I took the elevator down stairs to get the passport pictures. Again, it cost me. I went back to the floor, notify them that I was back and waited to be called. I was called back to the interviewer again.

She asked me the same questions about twenty times, "Why are you going to England and who told you about us?"

I gave her the same answer over and over again. Then, she informed me of the cost of the emergency passport, then the cost to order a new passport, plus shipment and delivery. I swallowed hard and paid the amount. Again, it cost me.

She then said something that startled me, "Your emergency passport will be ready tomorrow at 4 p.m."

I looked at her as if she had lost her mind, "Tomorrow at four! You don't understand my flight is leaving at 7 p.m. today. I cannot spend another day here. I would have to cancel my trip again, pay for another hotel fee and cab fee to go back and fort again. I have spent all the money I can spend."

"Who sent you here again, and how did you know about us?" she responded.

I sighed and repeated the whole dilemma to her again.

"What time did you say your flight leave again?" she asked.

"7 p.m.," I answered.

"O.k., go outside and wait until they call you. We actually close at five, do not leave. Give me your flight information and we'll see what we can do," she assured me.

I waited and waited until they closed the door at five and kept me inside. I was in anguish and total frustration. My flight is leaving at 7 p.m. It was then after 5 p.m. and I was not sure if I was going to get the passport. Then, I could not call London without having a calling card. At about 5:35 p.m. they called me and gave me an emergency pass port and told me to get to the airport as fast as I could. I thanked them and took the elevator down several floors, to catch a cab.

There were several cabs passing by and picking others up. I thought to myself, maybe I am not being aggressive enough. I did what the others were doing and still they were passing me by without acknowledgement. I didn't understand, and then I realize I was obviously being snubbed. I thought to myself, I have to get to the airport immediately and all these cabs are driving pass me.

I thought, "Oh God, please let one stop."

I glanced at my watch on occasion as time goes by sending me in desperation. Finally, one stopped and it was a Black cab driver and he asked me how long was I waiting. He was slightly irritated as he went off, on the unfairness of the cab drivers. At that point I did not care; all I wanted to do was to get to the airport on time.

My heart raced in anticipation, as we were caught in traffic. I told the driver I have to get there by 6:30. He told me not to worry he'll get me there on time. I don't know how we got out of that traffic, but I got there by 6:30 p.m. Again, it cost me. I ran to the locker to get my luggage, and then hurried upstairs to catch my flight.

My luggage was checked in on time, and I breathe a sigh of relief. As I was passing by an ATM machine, I withdrew $400.00. I walked a little further down and there was a money exchange place. I was about to walk by it, then something tells me to get some British pounds. I stopped, walked back and got 200 pounds then boarded my flight.

After all I've been through that day, I was deeply rewarded. I was sitting in coach and had to look around on several occasion to see if I was sitting in first class. I was on a Virgin Atlantic flight and it was magnificent.

I arrived in London in the morning and was literally looking around to see if anyone was there to pick me up. I did not notify anyone of my coming, but I thought that my mom and my aunt knew that my flight was re-scheduled for the same time, next day. I looked and looked and finally came to the conclusion that there was no one there to pick me up. First thing I did, was to get some British coins to call and see if anyone could pick me up, but the phone kept on ringing and ringing.

I panicked, here I am in a strange country and I have no clue where I am going and how to get there. Then, I remembered the other phone numbers and addresses my mom gave me at the airport. The next person I called was a relative of mine that we call Aunt Dolly. The last time I saw her, I was about five or six years old when she visited Jamaica. I was about thirty now.

The phone rang and a voice answered, "Hello!"

"Can I speak to Aunt Dolly please?" I asked.

"This is Dolly," she answered.

Gladly I said, "I don't know if you remember me, but...."

Before I could finish the sentence she said, "Sophie, of course I remember you."

Shocked! I said, "Well it's been so long I can't believe you remember me. Actually, I am at the airport and I tried to call grandma's house and the phone kept on ringing and ringing. I am stuck here and I don't know what to do."

She told me to stay put and she will see if her son could come and get me. From what I was gathering, she would have to get in touch with him. Who knows how long it would take, then, she would have to call me back. I had to think quickly, so I asked her if her address was the same address I had, and she agreed. Being in the Navy has taught me to be independent, so I told her I would take a cab to her address.

I boldly went outside with my luggage, show a cab driver the address and asked him if he could get me there. After looking at his map, we were on our way. He did not charge me a flat rate, the meter was turned on. I had no idea how far it was or where I was going. I just sat back, relaxed and was enjoying the ride.

After a somewhat long ride, I watched with precaution as the meter went up to forty, fifty, then sixty pounds. I started to worry and wondered how far do I have to go. I was not planning on spending all my British pounds and hoped I had enough to cover. Each time the numbers go up and up, my heart skipped a beat. By the time I reached my destination, it came up to over a hundred pounds. I was so glad, that I bought the pounds before I left the States.

Aunt Dolly was at the gate to meet me. She asked me if I needed help to pay for the taxi. I told her I had some pounds with me, so it is all taken care of. Relieved, I entered the house and put my bags down. She seems to know a lot about me, but I didn't know much about her. After giving me a tour of her house, she placed me at ease. We ended up sitting around the kitchen table.

"Your grandma tells me all about you," she said with an inquisitive smile.

I said in a surprising tone, "Really!"

"The hospital is close by here, and she would stop by and we would sit down right here and talk," she went on.

I sat there and listened as she gave me a brief history of her side of the family.

"Your grandma and I are first cousins, you know," she said.

I've often wondered why my mom called her Aunt Dolly.

"I even knew your great grandma," she uttered.

My interest was at its highest peak, "Really! You knew her."

"Of course I do! We all use to live in the same area in Jamaica. I still cannot forget the day that she kneeled, transfixed in the mud for a long time. Sometimes she would go for days without eating," she stated.

"Oh my gosh! Sometimes I fast like that too!" I responded.

We talked for a while until she beckoned her son to take me to the hospital to see my grandma. We arrived at the hospital, went up the elevators then towards her room, as my cousin led the way.

I entered the room and thought I was seeing a double. She looked just like my great grandma. My distant cousin quickly greeted my grandma and told her he had to go. There I was, staring at her. I noticed that her face was twisted on one side and she was indeed stiff, not to mention the fact that she was drooling from the side of her mouth. Instantly, I had a flashback of the dream I had, then I noticed she had a visitor who was trying to help her.

I acknowledge myself, "Hi, grandma! I don't know if you remember me but this is Sophia."

"Of course I remember you, you were here last night!" she responded.

"No! That wasn't me, it was Lorna and Jasmin, your daughters," I answered.

I know that Lorna and Jasmin were here yesterday, but you were here also," she responded.

I thought to myself that my grandma was loosing it, as I tried to correct her, "I was not here last night, I just got off the plane, then I took a cab to Aunt Dolly's house and her son, just took me here to see you."

"But you were here last night!" she said convincingly.

I did not say another word. I just pull up a chair and sat beside her. She introduced me to the visitor, who was a member of her church. She was drooling profusely so I took some napkins and wiped her mouth.

"Thank you darling," she muttered.

As I let her know that her response was welcomed, I noticed she was staring at me with a special glow in her face that startled me.

"Why are you looking at me like that, grandma? You're looking at me strangely," I asked.

"Because you were here last night," she responded.

Before I could respond the visitor said to her, "She looks different uh, you were expecting a little girl?"

Without my grandma taking her eyes off of me, she shook her head up and down in acknowledgement.

The visitor then said, "You see! Your grandmother had us looking all over the place for you. She had us looking under the bed, in the closet and in the hallway. She swore to God, you were here."

I was too exhausted to comprehend all of this. The last time I saw my grandma was at my great grandma's funeral, I was a grown adult. I just sat there in silence, until I noticed that her hair needed to be combed. Normally, I do not like to comb anyone's hair, but I asked for a comb and braided away. The visitor helped me to position her stiff body to reach the back of her head. When I was finished I reached over to the box of tissue to wipe her mouth, then I had a flash back about the dream I had, again. The visitor told her she was in good hands and left.

The nurse walked in the room to do her daily assessments and my grandma said to her, "Isn't today the 12th of March."

"Yes!" the nurse responded.

"The reason why I ask you, is because, my granddaughter and everyone seems to think that I am loosing it," she stated.

I quickly looked around the room to see if there was a calendar in the room or something with a date on it and could not find anything.

When the nurse left the room she said to me, "See! I'm not crazy."

Sitting by her side I made an assessment. Apparently, she had a stroke, her mouth was twisted and she was unable to move anything on the left side. That is why she had a stiffened appearance, but she was able to talk and move the parts on her right side. We continued to talk until my mom and aunt walked in. They were happy to see me. We were all talking when another visitor came in. He introduced himself and pulled up a chair.

We continued to talk, and then he asked, "Who is Sophia?"

I raised my hand slightly in acknowledgement.

"Thank God you are here! I thought she was dead for sure but she came out of it asking for you. She had us looking all over the place for you, she swore up and down that you were here!" he exclaimed.

I was slightly embarrassed, so I sat there in silence. The next visitor left and a close friend of the family walked in. Her name is Sonia, I had heard so much about her but this was my first time meeting her.

We sat down, talked and then she invited us to her house for dinner, "My mother would love to see you all."

When she walked out, my mom asked me, "Did you know that Miss Sissy is her mother?"

I was amazed. Miss Sissy was one of my great grandma's good friends. When I was a child, she was one of the folks we use to visit. I also found out that she was my Aunt Lorna's godmother. We stayed at the hospital for a while, but I was tired and hungry. We left around dinnertime and took a cab to Aunt Dolly's house. I had my first real fish and chips meal and it was great.

My luggage was still there so my Uncle Peter came by and drove us to where they lived. He was born and raised in England. The last time I saw him was when I was approximately five or six years of age, when they all visited Jamaica with Aunt Dolly.

We dropped my luggage off and went back to the hospital. When visiting time was over, we prayed with grandma and kissed her goodbye. We went back to the house and I was introduced to my uncle's wife and child. The next day we got up early and went to the marketplace close by. I bought a loaf of bread and a bottle of strawberry flavored syrup. When we got back, we went straight to the hospital.

Later we went back to the house. My mom and aunt went upstairs so I went in the kitchen. I was cutting off a slice of bread, when my uncle's wife walked in.

"Do you want me to fix you something?" she asked with her British accent.

"No, I'm not fussy. I'll just eat the bread and mix some syrup," I answered.

"Well, there is butter, jam and ice in the refrigerator if you need it."

"No thank you!" I uttered.

"You know, we were all afraid of you, then I spoke to Dolly and she told us you were a really nice person." She cautioned.

Finally, she struck up a conversation, which led me to tell her about the dream I had.

She said in shock, "Oh my God! I was there and the same thing you said, actually happened! We all thought that she was dead and we had her in the car and she was stiff. No wonder she was asking for you, oh my God!"

The next day we went to Sonia's house for dinner. I met her husband and kids and saw Miss Sissy. They had a feast prepared, accompanied with wine.

Sonia's husband said to me with a slight African accent, "So this is Sophia! Your grand mother was asking for you. She did not ask for the others, she only asked for you."

Again, I was slightly embarrassed, so I told them about the dream I had.

They were all amazed then Miss Sissy said, "You are just like your great grandma, she had dreams like that."

"She did? I asked.

"Yes! We were very close you know. We use to go all over when I was in Jamaica. They would send for her and she would go all over praying for the sick and they would get healed," she stated.

"Did you literally see them get healed?" I asked.

"Yes, of course! I was the one with her. She always let me read the Bible for her."

The next day we went to visit grandma in the hospital. I sat there and thought to myself that my grandma could be healed.

I said to her, "Miss Sissy told me about your mother. She said that they went all over healing people."

"Yes! She was the one to read the Bible for my mother," she answered.

"Do you believe in healing?" I asked.

"Yes!" she said convincingly.

"Then do you believe that God can heal you, in the name of Jesus."

"Yes!" she answered.

"Well, if you believe, raise your left hand," I stated.

To my amazement she raised her left hand, and had it up for a while and then she placed it back down. My mom was sitting across the room talking to one of her roommates. I quickly called my mom over and told her what had happened. We were all amazed. Her mouth was back to normal and she was not drooling as much.

As the time goes by, her skin began to clear up. Then I remembered Aunt Dolly saying that before her husband died, his skin had a certain glow to it. I sat there contemplating what I should do. Should I tell her she is healed and let her go back home, or take her back to the States?

As I sat there contemplating, her doctor walked in and he was amazed at her recovery. He told her that she should be ready now for another series of chemotherapy. The look on her face said it all, as the doctor left the room.

"Are you in pain grandma?" I asked.

"No! You don't understand. This illness is not a nice thing. It wears you down as if it is sucking the life out of you. I'm just tired; I can't go through with it any more. I am tired," she explained.

At that moment I understood what she meant.

"Are you at peace with yourself?" I asked.

"Yes," she answered.

"Is all well with your soul?"

Confidently she said, "Yes, darling."

Convinced, I said, "So! You already made your peace with God?"

She shook her head in acknowledgement and I totally understood. Our time in London was coming to an end and I tried to treasure the moments. On our last day, we did our hugs and kissed goodbye. We went back to the States. When the time came; my mom went on her trip to Israel.

While she was in Israel, I received a call that my grandma had passed away. My aunt and I made the decision not to inform her of her mother's passing until she returned to the United States. Going to Israel is a once in a lifetime experience and I did not want to interrupt her. Besides, she only had a couple of days left. Therefore, I went to the church and had them notify our pastor and have him not tell her what had happened.

In a couple of days my aunt and I went to get my mom from her trip and the pastor was very gracious to her. Then, she realized that something was wrong, by the looks on our faces.

She glanced at us both and said, "Is there something wrong, it's Mom uh?

"Yes! They called a couple of days ago and told us that she died," I answered.

She then said, "I knew it! You know when I realized it, I was at the Wailing Wall and I felt the presence of God upon me and I began to cry. Then, I wrote your names down on a piece of paper and I was praying for you all, while I was placing them in between the cracks. As I tried to place them in between the cracks one of them kept on falling out. Each time I would pick it up and stuff it back in, it would fall out. When I took a look, it was the one with Mom's name written on it."

My mom had to act quickly, she had little time. It was a good thing that her travel agent was also on the trip with them. She looked for her in the crowd, and then booked a flight immediately to go back to London. I could not attend the funeral. I felt very guilty and was thinking that I should have demanded her release and brought her back to the States.

My mom was devastated; she was weak so I had to be strong. The most important thing is we spent some quality time with her before she died. Sometimes we get selfish wanting to keep our loved ones around. It hurts, but do not forget, we all belong to the Father and not to each other. The choice is not ours; it is between them and their Creator. We cannot tell the body whether or not it should live forever. The soul belongs to the Lord.

I felt guilty, and then I remembered the conversation we had. She told me that she had made her peace with God and all was well with her soul. Then again, now that I thought of it, someone else would have died in her place. In the dream I had, when I carried her back into the house, she became loose as if she had a re-birth and someone else in the room became stiffened.

CHAPTER FIFTEEN

JESUS

As a child I had dreams and aspirations of becoming the first lady Prime Minister of Jamaica, with the intent of obtaining world peace. As I grew up and matured, I realized that I cannot save the world. The world was already saved. It was saved by Jesus Christ. Although the criteria are exclusive, everyone is still eligible to live in the confines of world peace.

This is why I call Him an equal opportunity God, because not even His Son was immune, in the fight against the plight of sin. It does not matter if you are the most dreadful, horrific danger to society. The offer is extended to all.

The serpent tricked Eve into partaking of the tree of knowledge of good and evil, which she also shared with her husband. When God found out He confronted them all, including the serpent. The serpent was first on the list, and God cursed it.

> "And I will put enmity between thee and the woman, and between thy seed and her seed; it shall bruised thy head, and thou shalt bruise his heel." (Genesis 3:15) KJV

The word enmity represents hatred, hostility and bad feelings. This is an on going battle that started from the beginning of time and still continues today. The battle is between the serpent's offspring and the offspring of Eve. The serpent's offspring represents evil and Eve's offspring represents good. This means that when Eve or any female produces an offspring, the chances are it is all in the genetics. One child could come out good, the other evil or one containing both genes.

Eve's first child is Cain and her second child is Abel. Cain was evil and Abel was good. Cain was jealous of his brother Abel and killed him. Evil survived and produced other offspring of the same genetics. Therefore, Eve had another child to replace Cain, named Seth. It took several generations to produce another good, which was Noah. Good and evil cannot mix; there will always be a constant battle. As long as evil exist we cannot live in peace. Sin became prevalent and inevitable as it passes through all the bloodlines.

In the book of Exodus the Lord instructed the people to build a place of worship to host the Spirit of God. They were to build an altar, so the people could offer gifts of sacrifice. An offer of sacrifice ranged from thanksgiving to forgiveness of sin. They would offer a burnt sacrifice of precious metals, animals, grain and baked goods.

> The offering is given to the priest, "And the priest shall make an atonement for him before the Lord: and it shall be forgiven him of anything of all that he had done." (Leviticus 6:7) KJV

The people made an offering of thanksgiving for the first fruits of the harvest. They knew that God was the Creator of all things on Earth, so they thanked him, by making an offering of sacrifice. When the people sin against the Lord, they offered a living animal sacrifice without blemish. The priest takes the animal's blood, sprinkles it on the altar, and then he burns a part of the meat as a sacrifice.

A sacrifice is a gift without any blemish, that's been purified and Holy in the eyes of God. It should not be unclean, marked or touched, but the best that you have to offer. God knew that man was prone to sin and offered a temporary solution. The solution became an agent of excuses than an agent of change, which further separated the people from God.

The people thought that they could do what ever they wanted to do, no matter how vile it is. After all, they will be forgiven. Does this sound familiar to you?

The people of today would use the term, "Once saved always saved."

We think we can do what ever we want to and we will not be responsible for our actions. Let's see what God had to say about their offerings of sacrifice.

"To what purpose is the multitude of your sacrifices to me? saith the Lord: I am full of burnt offerings of rams, and the fat of fed beast; and I delight not in the blood of bullocks, or of lambs, or of he goats." (Isaiah 1:11) KJV

The people thought that they were doing God a favor, instead of God doing them a favor to cover their sins. The major objection is to change, turn and seek. When we sin, the Spirit of God retreats and He hides his face from us. Then we become disconnected from the source of God.

Therefore, you are left exposed to the elements which are the antithesis of good. It then becomes a tug of war, with God holding on to you at one end, and the enemy holding on to you at the other end. Each time you sin the enemy pulls you closer and closer to his side.

When God cursed the serpent, he also mentioned some-thing that will bruise the serpent's head and the serpent will bruise his heel. What was He talking about? Before the feast of the Passover or as it is known as the Last Supper, Jesus shed some light on the text as He spoke to his disciples.

> "I speak not of you all: but that the scripture may be fulfilled, HE THAT EATETH BREAD WITH ME HATH LIFTED UP HIS HEEL AGAINST ME. Now I tell you before it come, that, when it is come to pass, ye may believe that I am he." (John 13:18, 19) KJV

Jesus was referring to Judas who would later betray Him, whom the devil had possessed. Several days prior to the feast, some of the disciples witness a strange phenomenon. They saw Mary poured an expensive ointment on Jesus and used her hair to wipe his feet. Can you imagine the thoughts that were going through their minds? First, they probably tried to reprimand her for what appear to be a waste at the time. Secondly, they probably thought that she was touching Jesus inappropriately.

Instead of asking Jesus the purpose of what was being done to him. They were quick to judge, causing their imagi-nations to run wild by speculating. Until this day some of us are still speculating. Judas interpreted it not only as a waste, but as a sin which prompted him to seek to betray Jesus. Jesus told them the truth that it was for the preparation for his burial. They did not understand at the time.

> "Yea, though I walk through the valley of the shadow of death, I will fear no evil: for thou art with me; thy rod and thy staff they comfort me. Thou preparest a table before me in the presence of my enemies: thou

anointest my head with oil my cup runneth over."
(Psalm 23:4, 5) KJV

There are books with rumors circulating about the authenticity of Jesus. They want to blemish the character of the Lamb of God. Jesus was a sacrificial gift from God. If Jesus was found to have caused himself to be blemished, he would have not been an acceptable sacrifice. Separate your facts from fiction; this is the perfect example of another man-made theory.

Then, there are others who like to blame others for the death of Jesus Christ. Some with their hatred and bigotry try to assign the blame on the Jews. Jesus knew exactly what to say and what not to say to stir up controversy. If you read the text, He was asked on many occasions if He was the true Messiah. Instead of revealing His true identity, He was very vague or did not answer the questions.

If Jesus had revealed Himself to them, would the prophecy be fulfilled? He was on an assigned task from God incognito. To reveal Himself, is to ruin the master plan. The most important thing was the devil knew He was there. God spoke the Word from the beginning and it was predestined. No one could have stopped the crucifixion except for the Word Himself.

God is a Spirit and the Words that he spoke from the beginning, helped him to manifest every thing that came to be. The Heaven and the Earth, the sun, moons and stars were manifested when God used His own Words. Therefore, the Word is also a Spirit because it came from God. When the glitch occurred in the Garden, God spoke the Word against the serpent to destroy the works of the devil.

Therefore, God found a host which is a direct bloodline from Abraham, whom God made a promise with. The Virgin Mary was the host that gave birth to the manifested Word of God. The manifested Word was given a name and His name is Jesus Christ. There are some who thinks that Jesus should not be exalted. They think He was just a man. It is not the man we exalt; it is the Word we exalt.

We love to give man credit for things that God have done. Don't blame the Jews when it was God's master plan. If that was the case I should be thanking the Jews instead of thanking God for sacrificing his Son. Those who blame the Jews are not only ignorant; they are unaware of God's master plan. Watch out for those that preach hate.

> "He that committeth sin is of the devil; for the devil sinneth from the beginning. For this purpose the Son of God was manifest that he might destroy the works of the devil." (1 John 3:8) KJV

Jesus was on assignment to preach, teach, testify and heal by demonstrating the power of God. In other words, the Word had to do and say what He heard from His Father. He reached out to people as a witness to the Kingdom of God and a testament to eternal life. God told us, not to sin yet we sin. Then God offers us the ultimate way out and some of us choose not to acknowledge His gift.

Why do we find it so hard to believe the Words of Jesus? Do you think that you are going to enter the Kingdom of Heaven in your present sinful state? The answer is, "No." You have to go through the rebirth process to enter the Kingdom of God.

> "Jesus answered and said unto him, verily, verily, I say unto thee, except a man be born again, he cannot see the kingdom of God." (John 3:3) KJV

When God first made man, they were spiritual beings. Adam and Eve sinned and became physical beings, meaning that they were disconnected from the source of God. In other words, they died spiritually. If we as a people want to see the Kingdom of God, we have to get back to Adam and Eve's original state. They were in God's protective custody.

"Go ye therefore, and teach all nations, baptizing them in the name of the Father, and of the Son, and of the Holy Ghost." (Matthew 28:19) KJV

Baptism is the rights of passage, giving rebirth to the flesh, which preserves you spiritually, that if you shed your earthly appearance, your spirit lives forever. How are your sins going to be forgiven if you do not accept the sacrificial Lamb of God? It would be an insult to God, if He offered you His very best, so that you can have eternal life, and you turn around and refuse to acknowledge His Son, Jesus Christ.

If you believe that Jesus sacrificed His life for you and me, as a sacrifice to God, so that we would be forgiven of our sins and obtains eternal life. Then, when we die an earthly death, we rose as He did in our spiritual form, so we can see the Kingdom of Heaven.

If you do not want to acknowledge Jesus, then you have no way of getting into the Kingdom of Heaven, because you have to go through Jesus to get to God. Remember, we are contaminated with sin; therefore we cannot be in the presence of God, in our sinful state. We have to cleanse ourselves of sin through the blood of the Lamb. Jesus is the intercessor of all men.

"Jesus saith unto him, I am the way, the truth and the life: no man cometh unto the Father, but by me. (John 14:6) KJV

This is why Jesus is worthy to be praised. He resisted all temptation, because He knows that if He succumbs to satan's devices, He would have sinned. If Jesus had sinned, He would have been unclean and therefore could not be sacrificed. Do you think that someone with Jesus courage should go unnoticed and unappreciated? The answer is, no. Isn't it God's willing to share His glory with Him. You can use your religion to deny Jesus, but the fact of the matter is.

"That at the name of Jesus every knee should bow, of things in heaven, and things in earth, and things under the earth; And that every tongue should confess that Jesus Christ is Lord, to the glory of God the Father." (Philippians 2:10, 11) KJV

Jesus came also to use himself as an example, to show us how to live. If we actually live the way, He told us to live, we would have world peace. We are so blinded by our appetite to appease the flesh that we literally cannot conceive, a spiritual order.

When Jesus was on Earth, he spoke in parables and was quite aware of the fact that, the majority of the people would not understand. This is the amazing thing about Jesus, with His intelligence and power; He could have persuaded everyone He came in contact with. If He did, the people would not fulfill the prophecy and have Him crucified. His main objective was to honor His commitment.

Jesus said, "For I came down from heaven, not to do my own will, but the will of Him that sent me." (John 6:38) KJV

Do you know how much self-control it takes, to know what it is like to be in Heaven, to know the Father personally, and the people are blind and clueless? It was frustrating, due to the fact that Jesus knows that He has a major competition. Instead of competing with His opponent, He outsmarted the adversary. Jesus used parables as a code, to be revealed only to those that believe in Him.

That is why there are so many unbelievers, the secrets of the codes have not been revealed to them. People are looking for proof and evidence, but it is only revealed to them that seek the Lord. You can continue to look in all the wrong places and you will never find God. Instead of digging up old bones and confusing a whole generation. How about, excavating the Bible and discovering the truth. Then again, can the blind see?

> Jesus said, "I am the living bread which came down from heaven; if any man eat of this bread, he shall live forever: and the bread that I will give is my flesh, which I will give for the life of the world." (John 6:51) KJV

To obtain eternal life, one has to partake of spiritual food. I once mention that spiritual food is the Word of God. The essential vitamins for spiritual food are belief, faith, baptism, praise, worship, prayers and the communion of bread and wine.

Jesus had His disciple partake of some spiritual food before He was crucified, at their last supper. They ate bread and wine, which represents the body and blood of Jesus Christ. Since the future generation was not around to witness the sacrifice of the Lamb of God. We were left with a legacy, a will and testament for our rights to forgiveness of sins. As an option, there is no need for animal sacrifices. To those that believe it is a simple puzzle, but to those that do not believe it is a complex piece of the puzzle.

> "For he is our peace, who hath made both one, and hath broken down the middle wall of partition between us. Having abolished in his flesh the enmity,

even the law of commandments contained in ordinances; for to make in himself of twain one new man, so making peace; And that he may reconcile both unto God in one body by the cross, having slain the enmity thereby: (Ephesians 2:15,16) KJV

When Jesus died on the cross, the hostility between the women's offspring and the serpent, are no longer applicable. We can sit, argue and fight amongst ourselves. There is Islam versus Judaism, versus Christianity, versus Hinduism, versus the Buddhist and so on and so on. Christianity is not immune, we also bicker amongst ourselves. We have the Catholic versus the Protestant versus the Baptist versus the Seventh Day Adventist and so on. It was predicted by God that there would be an enmity between us all. Therefore, God took away our rights to eternal life by barricading the tree of life.

With all our religions and denominations, we all claim to worship God, yet peace cease to exist.

We should all ask our selves, "Why?"

Is it all about God and obtaining eternal life or is it all about our obsession with the World, thinking that it is indispensible. Therefore, God provides us a mediator to bridge the gap amongst ourselves. He brought about peace that when we receive the Holy Spirit a new person is created. Therefore, we are reunited with God through Jesus.

"Little children, it is the last time: and as ye have heard that anti-Christ shall come, even now are there many anti-Christ; whereby we know that it is the last time." (1 John 2:18) KJV

CHAPTER SIXTEEN

THE HOLY SPIRIT

The Holy Spirit is the master activator that resurrects everything and makes it come alive. It was the same Spirit that was also with God in the beginning, when He created the Heaven and the Earth. In Genesis God made reference to, "us." He used the term in the plural sense, "Let us." Who do you think God was referring to, think about it? Did God created the Heaven and the Earth by Himself or did He embody the key principle alliance for His blueprint.

> "For there are three that bear record in Heaven, the Father, the Word, and the Holy Ghost: and these three are one." (1 John 5:7) KJV

In the chapter before, we have established the fact that Jesus represents the Word and is the Word. Everything that was made would have not been possible without the three. God spoke the Word with wisdom, the Word understood and with knowledge the Spirit brought it to life.

Before Jesus started His ministry, the first thing He had to do was to prepare Himself. Being made into a man, he had to go through the same process that is required of us today.

Jesus knew that He could not do it on His own, He needed help. Therefore, He had to be born again. The term, "Born Again," is synonymous with water and the Spirit. To be born again, water is used in the process as a form of baptism. It is an initiation through the purification of water and the birth of the Holy Spirit within you.

John the Baptist had the privilege of baptizing his cousin Jesus. It is written that the Spirit of God descended upon him like a dove and lightening. The rebirth process was complete, and then the product has to be tried and tested. This is when Jesus was lead into the wilderness for forty days and forty nights to be tried by the devil.

Jesus had to fast like every one else, including His fore fathers. With fasting He stayed connected to the source of God and was able to resist temptation. This is the same Spirit that lead, guided and directed His path when He started His ministry. It was also the same Spirit that cast out demons, healed the sick, and performed various miracles.

> Jesus said, "It is the spirit that quickeneth; the flesh profiteth nothing: the words that I speak unto you, they are spirit and they are life." (John 6:63) KJV

In other words our natural body is not immune from death and pain it is inevitable. Therefore, when we die we cannot exchange it for a life that is eternal. The flesh was made with the elements of the Earth and when it decomposes all that is left is the elements of the Earth. It is the Spirit that resurrects and makes all things alive and active.

Before Jesus died on the cross, He told his disciples that it was essential that He departed from them. They were not at all happy with His statements, even though it was beneficial for all of us. His departure was of extreme importance. The prophecy had to be fulfilled. We needed the blood of the lamb to take away the sins of the world. Then we needed peace in this world of chaos.

The Spirit of God was with Jesus the entire time except for when it was close to His departure. In the Garden of Gethsemane the Spirit of God left His body. There He was, exposed to the elements; He felt sad and lonely and needed company. The disciples were with Him but because of the wine from the Last Supper, they were not able to stay up with Him. Jesus did not partake of the wine with them. He assured them that he will not drink of the vine until He sees them in the Kingdom of Heaven.

The Spirit of God had to leave his body in order to raise Him from the dead. He was exposed to the element and in a moment of weakness He asked His Father for an alternation. Jesus knew the plan and made various predictions to His disciples, but His mind was willing but his flesh was weak. Then, the Word remembered it was not His will but the will of the Father.

> "So shall my word be that goeth forth out of my mouth: it shall not return unto me void, but it shall accomplish that which I please, and it shall prosper in the thing whereto I sent it." (Isaiah 55:11) KJV

There are some who challenge the Godliness of Jesus Christ. After all, He did display some moments of weakness and at a point on the cross He cried out and said, "My God, My God, why have thou forsaken me?"

You might be saying, "Is this suitable of a God?"

Jesus compared the process that he had to go through as to a woman in labor about to give birth. Before she goes into labor she knows and anticipates what is to come. When the time arrive, she dread going through the process because she knows what it entails. The anticipation of the pain, stress and trauma causes anxiety. It is overwhelming and she wishes there was another way out, yet she cannot change her mind. There she is, stuck with a burden to bear which is virtually inevitable. In the height of her deep distress she cries out in pain and agony. The baby is delivered; she goes from trauma to joy at the sight of her offspring.

The world with our sins, iniquities and transgressions were placed on His shoulders. When the burden was far too much to bear He called out to God in agony. Would a normal man possess such compassion and understanding especially with the circumstances that transpired leading to and on the cross? Jesus knows that His trauma would turn into joy. He was giving birth for all of us to obtain eternal life.

Instead, He told the ladies not to weep for him but to weep for themselves. Then, He asked God to forgive those responsible for His crucifixion for they did not know what they were doing. The Word knew that the Spirit would quicken His body, that He may complete his task and return unto the Father to reap His rewards.

> King David said, "I will worship toward thy holy temple, and praise thy name for thy lovingkindness and for thy truth: for thou hast magnified thy word above all thy name." (Psalm 138:2) KJV

Before Jesus went to be with His Father he spoke of things to come as a result of the trauma He went through. He spoke of His replacement that God will send in His name. Then he mentioned the baptism of the Holy Ghost. Judging by the way we still act and think you would assume that Jesus have abandoned us in a world of utter chaos with only a promissory note of His return. Yet we are left with a promise laying out a blueprint with infallible proofs as a witness of Jesus Christ.

The proofs are there, yet we choose to ignore it and act as if it does not exist. Do you think that it is because we do not understand it, or are we embarrassed by it? After all, it is not under our control, therefore it does not exist.

> Jesus said, "And I will pray the Father, and he shall give you another Comforter, that he may abide with you forever; Even the Spirit of truth; whom the world cannot receive, because it seeth him not, neither knoweth him: but ye know him; for he dwelleth with you, and shall be in you." (John 14:16-17) KJV

I remember as a child being invited to my neighbor's church, which was a Pentecostal affiliate. As I sat and observed, there were shouts of praise with people dancing. Some lost control of their bodies to the point where I had to move to get out of the way. They were a tambourine smacking, roof raising, Spirit filled and speaking in Tongues church.

I would look at them in my conservative manner and thought to myself, "How can they feel the Spirit and I can't?"

As soon as I arrive at home and was amongst my cousins, I explained what I witnessed by mimicking the way they danced or spoke. They all would laugh uncontrollably. On the serious side I was concerned because they possessed something that I could not feel or experience. Deep down inside I wanted to feel what they were feeling, yet I would be embarrassed by the loss of self control.

What they had was the baptism of the Holy Ghost. At that point in my life I did not have a water baptism and had no intention of giving my life to Christ. I was invited to churches of all denominations. The church I attended the most, was affiliated with my school and it was of the Catholic faith. The entire school had to attend Mass every Thursday whether or not you were a Catholic. It was a controlled environment, everyone was proper and had self control.

When I migrated to the U.S., I attended church with my mother. On occasion I witnessed a couple of people having a spiritual intervention, where they lost control of their bodies and speech. It got my attention and I know it was the work of the Lord. This was the same way that the folks in some of the churches in Jamaica acted. I became accustomed to the spiritual outbreaks as a custom of the church environment. Deep down inside I wanted to know what they were feeling, and then again I was glad it was them instead of me. I would have felt embarrassed to be on display in the midst of everyone.

After a great while of not attending church, I made the decision to go back and dedicate myself totally. My eyes were opened when I attended church with my mom. She lost control of herself and was dancing in the Spirit, I was shocked! My mom is always well dressed. I saw the care, time and effort she took. She would lay out her clothes and made sure that her hat, shoes and purse coordinated. Everything was in sync with its presentation. Hair and makeup was no exception. Now, I know that no one in their right frame of mind would go through all that process, and then act in a manner contrary to their personality.

I knew right then and there, it was not a fake. Then, I had my first encounter. The pastor told us to stand, raise our hands and receive the Holy Ghost. This time, I was receptive and wanted to move on to the next level. It was as if the wind blew over our hands and I felt a jolt of electricity that caused my hands to shake. Finally, I felt the Spirit of God that had eluded me all these years. I did not loose control spiritually, but that jolt was enough to convince me. I was overwhelmed with joy.

I thought that was it, when it was only the beginning. One Saturday I attended Morning Prayer service, which had a relatively small crowd. It started at 6 a.m., I do not remember precisely what transpired but I was overcome with the Holy

Ghost. My body felt as if it was on fire and I stood transfixed in the same spot without the ability to move about freely, shouting hallelujah continuously. I was rocking slightly from side to side. If I didn't know what was happening to me, I would think that I was being electrocuted.

It seemed like I experienced this for a while until I was able to move and I sat down but I could still feel the electricity all over my body and I could not stop saying, Hallelujah. There was a lady that came and sat beside me. She place one hand on my shoulder and one hand on her heart. Apparently, she had a heart condition and was praying for her heart. The following Sunday she stood in front of the congregation and told us that she had required heart surgery and a miracle took place and now the doctors told her she does not have to have surgery.

I was shocked at her announcement, yet I was happy for her and I praised the Lord. She did not mention placing her hand on me at the time and praying. After all, it was not me it was the Spirit of God. I had to learn how to humble myself. Remember, it is the Spirit that quickens; my normal body cannot do it on its own. After that, I kept my mouth shut, humbled myself and kept a low profile. A change was occurring in my life and I was not sure what was happening to me.

> "John answered, saying unto them all, I indeed baptize you with water; but one mightier than I cometh, the latchet of whose shoes I am not worthy to unloose: he shall baptize you with the Holy Ghost and with fire:" (Luke 3:16) KJV

Even though, I was privilege to witness the power of God I still had doubts. Next we had a guess minister who wanted us to receive the gift of speaking in Tongues. Many received the gift of Tongues on that day but I didn't. I thought that speaking in Tongues was a fake because I did not receive it. Several days later I spoke to a trusted friend of mine.

I ranted, "There is this lady minister that came to our church and she told us that her ministry is to go around to the various churches, teaching people how to speak in Tongues. I think it is a fake, how could people speak a different language that is not their native tongue. Don't you think it is fake?"

"No! It is not a fake," he answered.

"Do you know how to speak it?" I asked.

"Of course, I have spoken in Tongues," he remarked.

"You have! Then how comes I cannot speak it? I asked.

He said with assurance, "Just pray and ask God for the gift of Tongues and you'll see. You will get it."

After we got off the phone I lay in bed and prayed for the gift of tongues. Immediately, the tip of my tongue became tingly and heavy. As I continued to pray, I uttered words that were incomprehensive to me. As the days go by, whenever I started to pray, automatically I spoke in Tongues. My thoughts were in English but my tongue uttered another language. It was just as the lady minister told us, about it becoming our own personal prayer language that the devil cannot understand.

> "Likewise the Spirit also help with our infirmities: for we know not what we should pray for as we ought: but the Spirit itself maketh intercession for us with groaning which cannot be uttered." (Romans 8:26)

There are several degree of controversy pertaining to receiving the Holy Ghost and speaking in Tongues. Be not afraid or feel that you will embarrass yourself, take it to the next level. Observers for the first time may think that you are drunk, insane or a raving lunatic. When the Holy Spirit moves, no one can control their reaction to its presence. Some people run, dance, jump or simply pass out in the Spirit.

The Holy Spirit is what it is, a Spirit that we cannot see. How else is He going to get our attention or make His presence known also unto others? It is demonstrated through us, the believers of Jesus Christ. Instead of leaders trying to quench the Spirit and the speaking in Tongues, explain to the congregation what is happening. Do not prevent others from gaining access to spiritual growth because some may feel uncomfortable. Tell them that they are witnessing the power of God.

You must ask yourself this question, "Did Jesus die only for the forgiveness of my sins and my rights to eternal life?" The answer is, "No." Jesus did not leave us in utter chaos to suffer until His return. He prayed to the Father to give us a replacement, the Comforter which is the Holy Spirit. Remember the Spirit will not go contrary to the Word of God.

> "But the fruit of the Spirit is love, joy, peace, long-suffering, gentleness, goodness, faith, meekness, temperance: against such is no law." (Galatians 5:22-23) KJV

The Holy Spirit embodies perfection and is an advocate for good. As you know by now, there are two spirits and two voices. Therefore, one has to be very careful. We live in a world today, where it is hard to distinguish what is true. The Holy Spirit is our true witness of the Father and the Son.

There are lots of religious fanatics who are perpetrators that use religion to kill, rob and oppress. They are only in it for themselves or to further their cause, in the form of deception. You can see them on the news everyday. They incite nations to kill in the name of God. They hate in the name of God. They blow up abortion clinics in the name of God. They convince others to commit suicide in the name of God.

They are without the Holy Spirit so they do things that are contrary to the fruit of the Spirit. Their god is co-dependent on man, instead of man being co-dependent on their God. The God I serve takes on that responsibility Himself. That is why there is a judgment in the end. He doesn't have to recruit people with low self-esteem and lack of respect for life to take revenge for Him.

> "Dearly beloved, avenge not yourselves, but rather give place unto wrath: for it is written, Vengeance is mine; I will repay, saith the Lord." (Romans 12:19) KJV

When you listen to man's ideology and act upon them, you have made them your god. Therefore, they cannot promise you any real estate or anything that belongs to the Kingdom of God. This is the perfect example of how to distinguish the voice of a stranger. The Holy Spirit would not tell you to kill, hate and destroy yourself and others in the name of God. God is quite capable of avenging Himself.

The voice of a stranger will lead you astray. Jesus knew this, so He prayed very often. He also knew that it was not what He wanted to do, but what God wanted Him to do. There was a plan and purpose for His life.

> Jesus said, "Howbeit when he, the Spirit of truth, is come, He will guide you into all truth: for he shall not speak of himself; but whatsoever he shall hear, that shall he speak: and he will shew you things to come. He shall glorify me: for he shall receive of mine, and shall shew it unto you." (John 16:13-14) KJV

CHAPTER SEVENTEEN

GOD

When I finally decided to read the Bible in its entirety, the first book I read from start to end was Revelation. Being the impatient person that I was, had caused me to venture off into the final chapter. The violence and sense of doom was so disturbing. It was as if, I partake of a bitter concoction and couldn't spew it from my mouth.

I wondered, "Who is this God that people praise and talk about?"

After reading Revelation, I immediately formed my own opinions without prior knowledge of God. I thought He was vain, egotistical, violent and unfair."

When I look back at that time in my life, I do not regret my thoughts. It only wanted me to research, uncover and expose who this God really is. Why would He want to punish the church? Why send a host of attack on us? Why destroy the Earth and all its glory? What was the cause of all this needless pain and suffering? Most of all, what have we done to deserve this? I was puzzled and wanted to know. Because of not knowing and wanting to know caused me to come into the knowledge of Him.

After reading Revelation, I resorted to reading the start of the New Testament. There, I learned about a kind compassionate God who sent His Son to bear witness to the Kingdom of God. Jesus kept on reiterating the fact that He was not from this world and that His Father had sent Him. Then, Jesus demonstrated His love by sacrificing His life for us. I found out, there was an alternative route from my sense of doom.

Then, I resorted to reading the Old Testament of the Bible. There, I found out, how we ended up in this predicament. Imagine that, once unredeemable, now redeemable through the blood of Jesus Christ. Yet it is still a choice, you can accept Him or reject Him, take it or leave it.

"For God sent not His Son into the world to condemn the world; but that the world through Him might be saved." (John 3:17) KJV

God is Holy, Eternal, Righteous and the Everlasting Father. I could go on and on, but the only thing I have to say about God is, I am impressed, amazed and flabbergasted. At first, I thought God did not care, turned His back on us and inflict nothing but pain.

Until I established a relationship, that opened my eyes and force me to discover the truth. God is the Father of us all, a parental figure, yet gentle enough not to impose on our lives. We were all made by Him and for Him, in other words, we are private properties.

Most of you might say that you are your own person; nobody owns you and you do what ever you want to do. You are absolutely right, God respects each and every individual rights. We are made with a mind of our own, so we can choose. That is why I have grown to love God. I have the freedom of choice.

The reason why I stated that God is like a parental figure is, if you have a baby you are responsible for the baby until they are old enough to take care of themself. When your child is in your care, you are responsible for the teaching and molding of the child's character. Discipline is an important factor, whether they like it or not.

When the child turns into an adult and move out of your care, you no longer have jurisdiction over their lives. They are free to make their own decisions. If they are smart, they would keep in touch, ask for advice and prevent themselves from making major mistakes. If they do not want you to get involve in their lives, you have to respect their wishes. You cannot impose your own ideals on how they should live their lives, even though you do not like the way they choose to live it. You can only hope they do the right thing.

When God first made man and woman, He made them to make intelligent choices. Who would have thought that if they were given the choice to choose life over death, they would choose death? Even though satan deceived them, they fell for his device. It is still shocking, that many of us choose death over eternal life.

I have to stop writing my own will and allow the Holy Spirit to take over. God do not want me to sugar coat the image of the True and Living God. He does not want to be portrayed as being perfect, but Holy, Righteous, Faithful and Just. Like with all leaders you aim for perfection but, "Beware of the things with a mind of their own."

He is Holy, because He is the power that is. He is Righteous, because He is an advocate of good, and He is good. He is Faithful, because He is still with us. He is Just, because He is a God that is fair, and He is the ultimate Judge.

One night, I was lying in bed in the prostrate position. I felt an overwhelming force overtake me and I could not move. Being the fighter that I am, I struggled hard to move and couldn't. As I fought to gain control of my body I heard a voice crying which caused me to lay still and listen.

This is what I heard, "I want you to apologize to women for me, I made a mistake and...."

There is more but I have to explain. Eventually I was released and regained control of my body. I was shocked at what I heard, yet I felt empathy and understood. The crying was heart felt with extreme remorse. Again, I question myself about what I heard, why me and how am I going to relay a message without offending. I love God with all my heart and would never distort the image of God.

This is a part of writing this book that I must write even though it is not of my own will. I am appalled too myself. God admits that He made mistakes and mishandled certain situations. Since He is Just, He takes full responsibility and as a result of this, He will elevate women to new heights.

When God made us, He made man first. This shows us that He can create man, without us being born from a woman. Woman was made from man, so that man would not feel inadequate, because woman was to become the keeper of the birth of both male and female. This applies to the principle of being one in the Spirit of the Lord. God resides in Adam and Adam resides in Eve. Eve resides in Adam therefore God resides in Eve. If woman was made first, we would have assumed that, woman is the creator of man.

The Bible said, "Therefore shall a man leave his father and his mother, and shall cleave unto his wife: and they shall be one flesh." (Genesis 2:24) KJV

To become one flesh, apparently there should be the union of two equal halves. Where is there domination over the other? For one to dominate the other, they would be unequally yoked. They are not compatible with each other.

One would benefit while the other sacrifice in a relationship. This is the antithesis of God's intentions.

This is not my opinion, but God wants to apologize to women and takes full responsibility for their plight over the years. God was angry with Eve for partaking of the forbidden fruit, and sharing it with Adam. Not realizing the outcome would be so devastating over the years, God cursed women and before He knew it, it was spoken into existence. Those very Words still lie stagnant in the hearts of men.

This is the biggest slave trade know to humanity, the fight for the sole proprietorship of the female species. The enmity between the serpent and the woman still plaque the world. What a severe punishment?

"Unto the woman he said, I will greatly multiply thy sorrow and thy conception; in sorrow thou shall bring fort children; and thy desire shall be to thy husband, and he shall rule over thee." (Genesis 3:16) KJV

God realized this and made an equal sacrifice, the pain and suffering of His Son. Mary gave birth to Jesus and through Him, she was elevated and magnified. We are all one in the Spirit of the Lord, partners and fellow citizens.

If you dominate your helpmate, you are robbing them of their birthright to be equal in the Spirit of the Lord. If a man wants to be the head of the household and fail to recognize that God is the head of the household, the whole family is in trouble. If you want to lead, you better know the way.

"And God saw that the wickedness of man was great in the earth, and that every imagination of the thoughts of his heart was only evil continually. And it repented the Lord that he had made man on the earth, and it grieved him at his heart." (Genesis 6:5, 6) KJV

God actually regretted the fact that He created our very being. Can you imagine the pain, suffering and heartbreak, He has to endure. To witness man's appetite for destruction, spiraling out of control. God has to honor the right of man to choose, since He is a God of His Word, literally.

Then, He had to listen to the cries and pleas of the oppressed, begging Him to intervene. Challenging God, asking Him if He is not the God they and their forefathers have worshipped. God sends them a deliverer, who was equipped with powers unknown to man.

They were delivered through the demonstration of the power of God. Free to reap the benefits that God has to offer them. Judging by the way we currently are, they were sinful, filled with fear and doubt. God himself was scrambling, to find a solution to their sinful ways.

He made the Ten Commandments and hand delivered it Himself. Can you imagine the risk involved? They witnessed His power and glory, yet they continued to sin with fear and doubt. Even though they rebelled, God did everything in His power to gain and maintain their attention, without success. What is a God to do?

There are people who find it humiliating to serve God. When in actuality, God have been running behind us, cleaning up our mess, showing humility by serving us. This is love that is why I do not mind going to church, messing up my hairdo, sweating through my dress or risk twisting my ankle. I dance in the Spirit, wave my hands and praise the Lord. Guess what! I do not care who wants to see me and what they might say.

God have been reaching out to us, in spite of our contaminated foul manner. Most of us are waiting for a sign, for God to prove Himself. Why should He? To be humiliated again, by us turning around and doing the same things and most of all ignoring Him. We are the ones who broke the rule.

God acknowledges that we all make mistakes. That is why He provides us a way out. Now, you are practically being pleaded to, I am not going to plead with you. God do not need you, you need God. It is like God is speaking in vain. This is why He stops acknowledging us, go through His Son. There are rooms prepared for you, believe it or not, take or leave it.

"My covenant will I not break, nor alter the things that is gone out of my lips." (Psalms 89:34) KJV

These Words are trapped in time forever and it is the law. Have you ever said something that you wish you could take back, but the words were heard and trapped in the memories of time? Before you know it, the words created a cause and effect. The difference with God and us is that the Word of God is. Once the Word is formulated and comes out of His lips, and so be it.

Notice that when God made the commandments, laws and promises, He did not say that man is going to obey them and do as I say. God created the Heaven and the Earth, which exist and strive on instinct. You do not have to tell the Sun to rise, the Moon to shine, the rain to fall, the grass to grow, the animals to eat etc. When God spoke, they knew their assigned job and purpose.

Try telling a cow that its purpose here on Earth is to fly. You will get no where. The cows know their purpose, because it is trapped in time. We have the capability to make a choice of our own, if we want something; we have to make it happen. Humans do not have wings to fly. We make objects to fly in.

Some of us obtain the promises of God through faith, by believing. Once you receive the promises of God, no one can take it away from you, not even God Himself. The only reason why satan is alive is because he is under the Covenant of God. God promises that if we partake of the tree of life, we will live forever. The tree of life is off limit for us, but satan ate from the tree of life first, then He committed the acts of sin.

This goes to show you, that when God makes a promise, it is His Word. When satan figured that he could do whatever he wants, because he is going to live forever, he changed. We do the same thing, once we are under a contract. We do what we want to do. Most of us fall in love, get married and made promises to each other, to death do you part. This is a contract of agreement.

For example God promises you an island and hands it over to you. Instead of following God's Commandments, you do whatever you want to do, becoming selfish because it is your island. Soon, you forget about God and His principles and incorporated your own. Obviously, you are going to get disconnected from the source of God. Now, you are left exposed to the elements putting others at risk. The natives become aware of this and kick you off the island. The island could have been yours, but you lost it because you became a victim of your own choice.

Instead of a sinner trying to outsmart God, with God's own Words, they in turn become victims by not keeping His Commandments. Therefore, God keeps His Words and promises.

"For the wisdom of this world is foolishness with God. For it is written, He taketh the wise in their own craftiness." (1 Corinthians 3:19) KJV

Satan and his followers thought that they could outsmart God, since they already partake of the tree of life. They also know that God was true to His Word. Can you imagine the thoughts that were going through their minds? They probably were thinking that they could do whatever they want to do, because they are guaranteed eternal life.

What is a God to do? If He destroys satan and his followers, this means that He is not true to His Word. If He allows them to roam free, they would cause a major catastrophe. The most ironic thing is we have power and authority over all demonic forces. Instead of entertaining God, most of us entertain these forces. We allow ourselves to succumb to things that are not of God.

Fortunately, God outsmart satan, He kept His Word by letting satan have eternal life. God is going to lock him away for one thousand years, release him then ultimately destroys his body and soul forever. If you were satan and you know what lies ahead in your future, would you go away quietly without a stir, especially if you are free?

I am not proclaiming perfection, after you have made a decision. Let us be realistic, nothing on this entire Earth is perfect. In some areas, it is too cold or too hot. If you find the perfect weather, watch out for earthquakes, hurricane, typhoon, etc.

A rose is one of the most beautiful and well known flowers in the world, but it has a menacing flaw, "thorns." Bees are a busy creature that makes one of the sweetest substances, known to man. If their handy work is interrupted, you could get stung to death. I could go on and on. This is how awesome God is; it is a reminder of His boundless creativity and power. The perfect place is what God have prepared for us.

You can start by attending a church of your choice. Let me stress this; do not go looking for perfection! The Holy Spirit is the embodiment of perfection. It teaches, corrects and modifies our abnormal behavior patterns. We are all on different levels on our way to being perfected.

There are several denominations, but there is, "One Lord, one faith, one baptism: One God and father of all, who is above all, and through all and in you all." (Ephesians 4:5, 6) KJV

As far as selecting a church, I recommend one that acknowledges Jesus. If you do not have the Lamb of God, how are you going to enter into the Kingdom of Heaven? Your number one priority is your relationship with God. Do not worry about what the pastors does in there spare time or even its members. You go to church to fellowship with God.

Do not, by any means, let anything or anyone get in your way, on the path to finding God. You will find some person-alities in the churches, who have not taken on the character of God. Their job is to deter you, from obtaining the prom-ises of God.

"He that hath an ear, let them hear what the Spirit saith unto the churches; To him that overcometh will I give to eat of the tree of life, which is in the midst of the paradise of God." (Revelation 2:7) KJV

My final advice to you is, "Beware of satan's devices."